AI4 Corporations
Volume III

Navigating AI Compliance with Confidence

Jamie Culican

Melle Melkumian

Published by Dragon Realm Press

Cape May Court House, New Jersey, USA

www.dragonrealmpress.com

AI-Enabled Technology was utilized in collaboration when creating this series.

Printed in the USA

First Edition: May 16, 2023

CONTENTS

INTRODUCTION

EMBRACING AI COMPLIANCE: SETTING THE STAGE FOR SUCCESS IN THE AGE OF ARTIFICIAL INTELLIGENCE

IN THE RAPIDLY EVOLVING WORLD OF ARTIFICIAL intelligence (AI), businesses find themselves navigating a complex and dynamic landscape. With AI transforming industries and redefining the way we work, there is a growing need for organizations to establish robust compliance frameworks that ensure responsible and ethical AI deployment. As an AI expert professional, my goal is to guide you through the intricacies of AI training and compliance, and empower your organization to harness the full potential of AI technologies while mitigating risks.

In this introductory section, we will lay the foundation for understanding the importance of AI compliance in today's business landscape. With the advent of AI, new legal, ethical, and regulatory challenges have emerged, necessitating a comprehensive approach to compliance that goes beyond traditional boundaries. By developing a culture of AI Compliance Excellence, your organization can not only protect itself from potential liabilities but also gain a competitive advantage in the marketplace.

Throughout this book, we will delve into the critical components of an effective AI compliance strategy, from building a tailored policy framework to implementing engaging employee training programs. We will also explore special considerations in AI compliance, such as industry-specific requirements, global legal considerations, and the unique challenges faced by public sector organizations. By understanding the importance of adaptability, continuous improvement, and collaboration, your organization can stay ahead of the curve as AI continues to reshape the business landscape.

As we embark on this journey together, it is my hope that you will find this comprehensive guide an invaluable resource for achieving AI Compliance Excellence. By embracing AI compliance as a strategic priority, your organization can unlock the full potential of AI technologies while navigating the complex world of AI governance with confidence and foresight. Welcome to the future of AI compliance, where responsible innovation meets business success.

Navigating the New Frontier: The Crucial Role of AI Compliance in Today's Business World

As artificial intelligence (AI) continues to permeate the modern business landscape, organizations must prioritize AI compliance to safeguard their interests and maintain a competitive edge. The importance of AI compliance cannot be overstated, as it serves as the bedrock for responsible and ethical AI adoption, ensuring that organizations remain aligned with legal and regulatory requirements while minimizing potential risks.

In an age where AI-driven solutions are transforming industries and revolutionizing the way we work, businesses that fail to address AI compliance proactively may face significant consequences. These can range from costly fines and legal disputes to reputational damage and loss of trust among customers, partners, and stakeholders. Moreover, non-compliant AI systems may inadvertently perpetuate biases or infringe upon individual privacy rights, leading to ethical dilemmas and public backlash.

By prioritizing AI compliance, organizations can foster a culture of responsibility and accountability that extends from the C-suite to individual employees. This commitment to compliance excellence not only mitigates risks but also contributes to the establishment of industry best practices and the development of a sound AI governance framework. In doing so, companies can position themselves as leaders in the ethical use of AI, ultimately enhancing their brand image and fostering customer trust.

Furthermore, a proactive approach to AI compliance enables organizations to stay abreast of the ever-evolving regulatory landscape. As governments and regulatory bodies around the world grapple with the implications of AI, new guidelines and legislation are continually being introduced to address emerging concerns. Companies that prioritize compliance are better equipped to adapt to these changes and incorporate them into their AI policies and practices, ensuring long-term success in a dynamic business environment.

The importance of AI compliance in the modern business landscape cannot be overstated. By embracing AI Compliance Excellence, organizations can navigate the complex world of AI governance with confidence, ensuring that their AI-driven solutions are both legally compliant and ethically sound. As we continue to push the boundaries of what AI can achieve, businesses must remain vigilant and proactive in their compliance efforts, paving the way for a future in which AI innovation is guided by responsibility and foresight.

AI Compliance Excellence: The Gold Standard for Responsible and Ethical AI Adoption

The rapid expansion of artificial intelligence (AI) across industries presents organizations with both unprecedented opportunities and formidable challenges. To navigate this new frontier successfully, businesses must strive for AI Compliance Excellence, a holistic approach to AI governance that encompasses legal, regulatory, ethical, and social dimensions. This concept represents the gold standard for responsible AI adoption and serves as a guiding principle for organizations seeking to balance innovation with accountability.

AI Compliance Excellence is built upon a foundation of proactive and comprehensive compliance strategies that address the unique concerns of AI technologies. By taking a proactive approach, organizations can ensure that their AI systems are developed, implemented, and monitored in alignment with relevant laws, regulations, and ethical guidelines. This commitment to compliance not only minimizes potential risks and liabilities but also enables businesses to harness the transformative power of AI in a responsible and sustainable manner.

At the core of AI Compliance Excellence lies a focus on continuous improvement and adaptability. As the AI landscape continues to evolve, so too must an organization's compliance efforts. This requires an ongoing commitment to refining policies, updating training programs, and staying informed of emerging trends and developments. By fostering a culture of learning and collaboration, businesses can ensure that their AI compliance initiatives remain agile and responsive to the dynamic world of AI governance.

Moreover, AI Compliance Excellence calls for a comprehensive approach that extends beyond legal and regulatory compliance to encompass ethical considerations and social impact. This means that organizations must not only adhere to existing laws and regulations but also proactively assess and address the broader implications of their AI technologies. By taking a principled and human-centric approach to AI compliance, businesses can ensure that their AI systems are designed and deployed in a manner that respects individual rights, promotes fairness, and fosters trust among stakeholders.

In summary, AI Compliance Excellence represents the pinnacle of responsible AI adoption in the corporate world. By embracing this concept, organizations can navigate the complex landscape of AI governance with confidence, ensuring that their AI-driven solutions are not only legally compliant but also ethically sound and socially responsible. As we continue to explore the vast potential of artificial intelligence, AI Compliance Excellence will serve as a beacon, guiding businesses toward a future in which innovation and accountability go hand in hand.

CHARTING THE COURSE: AN OVERVIEW OF OUR JOURNEY TOWARD AI COMPLIANCE EXCELLENCE

As we embark on this exploration of AI training and compliance, our goal is to provide organizations with the knowledge and tools necessary to achieve AI Compliance Excellence. This comprehensive guide will delve into the essential components of an effective AI compliance strategy, offering insights, best practices, and actionable recommendations for businesses seeking to navigate the complex world of AI governance. By following this roadmap, organizations can ensure that their AI-driven solutions are both legally compliant and ethically sound, paving the way for sustainable innovation and success.

The book is structured in two parts, each addressing distinct aspects of AI compliance. In Part One, we will focus on the foundations and strategies for achieving AI Compliance Excellence. We will cover the critical components of an effective AI compliance program, including building robust corporate compliance policies, designing engaging training modules for employees, and implementing proactive monitoring and check-ins. We will also discuss the importance of staying informed through intelligence reports, fostering a mindset of continuous improvement, and collaborating with industry peers and regulatory bodies.

Part Two delves into special considerations in AI compliance, addressing unique challenges and opportunities presented by specific contexts and industries. We will explore topics such as mergers and acquisitions, global legal considerations, industry-specific compliance requirements, and public sector AI compliance. Additionally, we will examine the future of AI compliance, emerging trends and technologies, and the importance of measuring the impact of AI Compliance Excellence on your organization's overall performance.

Throughout the book, we aim to provide readers with a comprehensive understanding of AI compliance and its implications in the modern business landscape. Our objectives include:

1. Equipping organizations with the knowledge and tools necessary to develop and implement effective AI compliance strategies.
2. Promoting a culture of AI Compliance Excellence that balances innovation with responsibility and accountability.
3. Encouraging continuous improvement, adaptability, and collaboration in the ever-evolving world of AI governance.
4. Addressing unique challenges and opportunities presented by specific industries, contexts, and regulatory landscapes.
5. Empowering businesses to assess the effectiveness and impact of their AI compliance initiatives and identify areas for growth and development.

By providing a comprehensive and actionable guide to achieving AI Compliance Excellence, we hope to empower organizations to harness the full potential of AI technologies while navigating the complex world of AI governance with confidence and foresight. Together, we can chart a course toward a future in which AI-driven innovation is guided by responsibility, ethical considerations, and a commitment to excellence in compliance.

BEYOND THE LAW: ETHICAL CONSIDERATIONS AND THEIR INFLUENCE ON AI COMPLIANCE

While legal and regulatory compliance is undeniably crucial in the realm of artificial intelligence (AI), businesses must also acknowledge the significance of ethical considerations in shaping AI governance. Ethics play a pivotal role in AI compliance, as they inform the responsible development and deployment of AI systems and help ensure that these technologies align with societal values, foster trust, and promote fairness.

Ethical considerations in AI compliance extend beyond adherence to laws and regulations, addressing the broader implications and consequences of AI-driven solutions. As AI technologies become increasingly integrated into our lives, organizations must grapple with complex ethical questions that influence their AI compliance efforts. Some key ethical concerns include:

1. Bias and fairness: AI systems can inadvertently perpetuate existing biases or create new ones, leading to unfair treat-

ment of certain groups or individuals. Organizations must prioritize the development of unbiased AI models and implement transparent algorithms to promote fairness and prevent discrimination.

2. Privacy and data protection: The collection, storage, and processing of personal data are integral to many AI applications, raising concerns about privacy and data security. Businesses must implement robust data protection measures, respect user consent, and ensure that their AI systems comply with applicable data privacy regulations.

3. Transparency and explainability: As AI models grow increasingly complex, understanding their decision-making processes becomes more challenging. Organizations should strive for transparency and explainability in their AI systems, enabling users to understand the rationale behind AI-generated outcomes and fostering trust in the technology.

4. Accountability and responsibility: Determining accountability for the actions and decisions made by AI systems can be complex. Companies must establish clear lines of responsibility and implement mechanisms for addressing potential harm caused by AI technologies, ensuring that they are held accountable for their AI systems' actions.

5. Human-centric design: AI systems should be designed with human values and well-being in mind. Organizations must prioritize human needs, rights, and dignity in the development and deployment of AI technologies, ensuring

that these systems enhance human capabilities and
autonomy rather than diminishing them.

By addressing these ethical considerations, businesses can
develop AI systems that are not only legally compliant but
also morally sound and socially responsible. The integration
of ethics into AI compliance efforts helps foster trust among
stakeholders, enhances brand reputation, and ultimately
contributes to the long-term success of an organization in the
AI-driven world. By prioritizing ethical considerations in their
AI compliance strategies, businesses can navigate the complex
landscape of AI governance with confidence, ensuring that
their AI-driven solutions align with societal values and
promote a future where technology serves the greater good.

The Pillars of AI Compliance Excellence: Foundational Elements for Responsible AI Governance

In the pursuit of AI Compliance Excellence, organizations
must establish a solid foundation built on key principles that
guide their AI governance efforts. These pillars of AI
Compliance Excellence not only ensure adherence to legal
and regulatory requirements but also promote the ethical
and socially responsible development and deployment of AI
systems. By understanding and implementing these foundational elements, businesses can navigate the complex land-

scape of AI governance with confidence and foresight, paving the way for sustainable innovation and long-term success.

The Pillars of AI Compliance Excellence encompass several crucial components, each playing a vital role in shaping a comprehensive and proactive AI compliance strategy. These elements, which will be explored in detail throughout this book, include:

1. Expert consulting and guidance: Engaging knowledgeable AI compliance experts and advisors can provide organizations with valuable insights, recommendations, and best practices, enabling them to navigate the evolving regulatory landscape and address AI-specific compliance challenges effectively.

2. Routine compliance check-ins and monitoring: Regular assessments and monitoring of AI systems help organizations identify compliance gaps, address potential violations, and ensure that their AI-driven solutions continue to meet legal, regulatory, and ethical requirements.

3. Intelligence reports on industry trends and regulatory updates: Staying informed of emerging trends, technological advancements, and new regulations is essential for businesses seeking to maintain AI Compliance Excellence. Intelligence reports can provide organizations with timely updates and insights, allowing them to adapt their compliance strategies accordingly.

4. Ongoing policy and training program refinements: As the

world of AI continues to evolve, so too must an organization's AI compliance policies and training programs. By embracing a culture of continuous improvement and adaptability, businesses can ensure that their compliance efforts remain agile and responsive to changing circumstances.

By incorporating these foundational pillars into their AI compliance strategies, organizations can achieve AI Compliance Excellence, balancing innovation with accountability and responsibility. This comprehensive approach to AI governance helps businesses mitigate risks, foster trust among stakeholders, and ultimately unlock the full potential of AI technologies in a manner that aligns with societal values and expectations. As we explore these pillars in greater detail throughout this book, organizations will be equipped with the knowledge and tools necessary to build a robust and proactive AI compliance strategy, paving the way for a future in which AI-driven innovation is guided by responsibility and foresight.

HARNESSING EXPERTISE: THE ROLE OF EXPERT CONSULTING AND GUIDANCE IN AI COMPLIANCE EXCELLENCE

In the rapidly evolving world of AI, organizations face unique challenges and complexities when it comes to compliance. To effectively navigate the AI governance landscape, businesses must seek expert consulting and guidance from professionals with specialized knowledge and experience in AI compliance. Engaging these experts can provide organizations with invaluable insights, recommendations, and best practices, empowering them to develop and implement AI compliance strategies that are both effective and sustainable.

Expert consultants possess a deep understanding of the legal, regulatory, ethical, and technical aspects of AI governance. Their expertise enables them to identify potential compliance risks and offer tailored solutions that address an organization's specific needs and objectives. By leveraging their knowledge, businesses can ensure that their AI-driven initiatives are compliant with relevant laws and regulations while also adhering to ethical principles and societal expectations.

Moreover, expert consulting and guidance can help organizations stay informed of emerging trends, technological advancements, and new regulations in the AI space. As the regulatory landscape continues to evolve, expert consultants can provide timely updates and insights, allowing businesses to adapt their compliance strategies accordingly. This proactive approach to AI governance helps organizations minimize risks, avoid potential liabilities, and maintain a competitive edge in the AI-driven world.

In addition to providing strategic guidance, expert consultants can also assist with the practical aspects of AI compliance, such as developing robust corporate policies, designing effective training programs, and implementing monitoring and reporting mechanisms. By offering comprehensive support and resources, expert consultants can empower organizations to build a solid foundation for AI Compliance Excellence.

Expert consulting and guidance play a crucial role in achieving AI Compliance Excellence. By engaging knowledgeable professionals with specialized expertise in AI governance, organizations can develop and implement comprehensive and proactive AI compliance strategies that mitigate risks, promote ethical and responsible AI adoption, and ultimately drive long-term success in the AI-driven business landscape.

STAYING VIGILANT: THE IMPORTANCE OF ROUTINE COMPLIANCE CHECK-INS AND MONITORING IN AI GOVERNANCE

As AI technologies become increasingly integrated into business operations, maintaining AI Compliance Excellence requires a proactive and continuous approach to compliance management. Routine compliance check-ins and monitoring play a pivotal role in ensuring that AI-driven solutions remain aligned with legal, regulatory, and ethical requirements while mitigating potential risks and liabilities. By regularly assessing and evaluating AI systems, organizations can identify compliance gaps, address potential violations, and make timely adjustments to their AI compliance strategies.

Routine compliance check-ins involve regular audits and reviews of an organization's AI systems, policies, and practices. These check-ins can help identify areas where improvements or updates may be necessary, allowing businesses to refine their AI compliance strategies and adapt to evolving regulations and industry standards. By conducting routine check-ins, organizations can proactively address potential compliance issues, minimizing the risk of legal penalties and reputational damage.

Monitoring plays a complementary role in AI compliance management, focusing on the ongoing analysis and assessment of AI systems' performance, behavior, and outputs. Implementing AI-powered monitoring and analysis tools can enable organizations to identify compliance gaps and potential violations in real-time, allowing for prompt remediation and adjustments. By continuously monitoring AI systems, businesses can ensure that their AI-driven solutions consistently adhere to compliance requirements and ethical principles.

In addition to promoting AI Compliance Excellence, routine compliance check-ins and monitoring can also offer valuable insights into the effectiveness and impact of an organization's AI-driven initiatives. By evaluating AI systems' performance against established benchmarks and objectives, businesses can identify areas for improvement, optimize resource allocation, and maximize the return on investment in AI technologies.

In summary, routine compliance check-ins and monitoring are essential components of a proactive and sustainable AI compliance strategy. By regularly assessing and evaluating AI systems, organizations can maintain AI Compliance Excellence, mitigate risks, and ensure that their AI-driven solutions continue to meet legal, regulatory, and ethical requirements. In the fast-paced world of AI, staying vigilant and proactive in compliance management is key to unlocking the full potential of AI technologies and driving long-term success in the AI-driven business landscape.

Staying Informed: Leveraging Intelligence Reports on Industry Trends and Regulatory Updates for AI Compliance Excellence

In the rapidly evolving world of AI, staying informed of industry trends, technological advancements, and regulatory updates is crucial for organizations striving for AI Compliance Excellence. Intelligence reports serve as a valuable resource, providing timely and comprehensive information that enables businesses to adapt their AI compliance strategies, respond to emerging challenges, and capitalize on new opportunities.

Intelligence reports offer insights into the latest developments in AI technologies, applications, and use cases. By staying informed of these trends, organizations can better understand the potential risks and benefits associated with specific AI implementations, allowing them to make informed decisions about the adoption and integration of AI-driven solutions. This proactive approach to AI governance helps businesses maintain a competitive edge while ensuring that their AI initiatives align with legal, regulatory, and ethical requirements.

Regulatory updates, another vital component of intelligence reports, keep organizations informed of changes in AI-related laws and regulations. As the regulatory landscape for AI continues to evolve, staying abreast of these updates is essential for maintaining AI Compliance Excellence. By keeping up to date with new regulations and guidelines, businesses can adapt their AI compliance strategies accordingly, minimizing the risk of legal penalties and reputational damage.

Moreover, intelligence reports can also provide insights into best practices, case studies, and lessons learned from other organizations' experiences with AI compliance. By learning from industry peers and regulatory bodies, businesses can refine their AI governance strategies, identify potential pitfalls, and adopt proven approaches to AI compliance management.

Intelligence reports on industry trends and regulatory updates are invaluable resources for organizations seeking AI Compliance Excellence. By staying informed of the latest developments in AI technologies, applications, and regulations, businesses can develop and implement agile, responsive, and effective AI compliance strategies. By embracing a proactive approach to AI governance, organizations can navigate the complex landscape of AI compliance with confidence, ensuring that their AI-driven solutions remain aligned with legal, regulatory, and ethical requirements while driving long-term success in the AI-driven business landscape.

Embracing Adaptability: The Significance of Ongoing Policy and Training Program Refinements in AI Compliance Excellence

The dynamic nature of AI technologies and the evolving regulatory landscape require organizations to adopt a flexible and adaptive approach to AI compliance management. Ongoing policy and training program refinements are essential components of AI Compliance Excellence, ensuring that organizations' AI governance strategies remain agile and responsive to changing circumstances. By continuously updating and refining their AI compliance policies and training programs, businesses can effectively manage risks, foster a culture of compliance, and ensure the responsible development and deployment of AI-driven solutions.

AI compliance policies provide the framework for an organization's AI governance efforts. As new regulations emerge and industry standards evolve, organizations must regularly review and update their policies to ensure alignment with legal, regulatory, and ethical requirements. This ongoing refinement process enables businesses to proactively address potential compliance gaps, minimize risks, and maintain a competitive edge in the AI-driven world.

Training programs play a crucial role in cultivating a culture of compliance and fostering employee awareness and understanding of AI compliance requirements. Regularly reviewing and updating training programs ensures that employees remain informed of the latest developments in AI technologies, applications, and regulations, empowering them to make responsible decisions and contribute to the organization's AI Compliance Excellence. By incorporating interactive and engaging training modules, businesses can encourage continuous learning and promote employee engagement in AI compliance initiatives.

Moreover, ongoing refinements to policies and training programs enable organizations to incorporate insights gained from routine compliance check-ins, monitoring, and intelligence reports. By leveraging these valuable resources, businesses can identify areas for improvement, optimize their AI governance strategies, and ensure that their AI-driven initiatives continue to meet legal, regulatory, and ethical requirements.

In summary, ongoing policy and training program refinements are integral to achieving AI Compliance Excellence. By embracing adaptability and continuously updating their AI compliance strategies, organizations can navigate the complex and ever-changing landscape of AI governance with confidence. This proactive approach to AI compliance management fosters a culture of responsibility, mitigates risks, and ultimately drives long-term success in the AI-driven business environment.

FINAL THOUGHTS

As we conclude this chapter, it is evident that achieving AI Compliance Excellence is a multifaceted endeavor that requires a proactive, adaptive, and comprehensive approach to AI governance. By understanding and implementing the foundational pillars of AI Compliance Excellence, organizations can navigate the complex landscape of AI compliance with confidence, fostering responsible innovation and driving long-term success in the AI-driven business environment.

The key principles explored in this chapter, including expert consulting and guidance, routine compliance check-ins and monitoring, intelligence reports on industry trends and regulatory updates, and ongoing policy and training program refinements, are essential components of a robust and proactive AI compliance strategy. By incorporating these elements into their AI governance efforts, organizations can ensure that their AI-driven initiatives align with legal, regulatory, and ethical requirements, mitigating risks and fostering trust among stakeholders.

As the world of AI continues to evolve at an unprecedented pace, embracing AI Compliance Excellence is not only a matter of adhering to regulations but also a vital component in driving sustainable innovation and growth. By maintaining a strong focus on AI compliance, organizations can unlock the full potential of AI technologies, capitalize on new opportunities, and ultimately contribute to a future in which AI-driven solutions are guided by responsibility, foresight, and ethical considerations.

As we delve deeper into the various aspects of AI compliance in the subsequent chapters, organizations will be equipped with the knowledge, tools, and best practices necessary to build a comprehensive and effective AI compliance strategy. The journey toward AI Compliance Excellence is an ongoing one, but with a solid foundation in place, organizations can confidently navigate the complex world of AI governance and shape a future that balances innovation with accountability and responsibility.

CHAPTER 1

LAYING THE GROUNDWORK: CRAFTING A ROBUST AI CORPORATE COMPLIANCE POLICY

AS AI TECHNOLOGIES BECOME AN INTEGRAL PART OF modern business operations, developing a robust AI corporate compliance policy is crucial to ensure responsible innovation and mitigate potential risks. A strong AI compliance policy serves as the foundation for an organization's AI governance efforts, guiding the development, deployment, and management of AI-driven solutions in alignment with legal, regulatory, and ethical requirements. This section introduces the key steps and considerations involved in building a comprehensive and effective AI corporate compliance policy, empowering organizations to navigate the complexities of AI compliance with confidence and diligence.

A robust AI compliance policy addresses various aspects of AI governance, including data privacy and security, algorithmic fairness and transparency, and accountability for AI-driven decisions. By establishing clear guidelines and expectations for AI development and deployment, organizations can foster a culture of compliance and responsibility, ensuring that AI-driven solutions adhere to legal, regulatory, and ethical standards.

Creating a comprehensive AI compliance policy requires a deep understanding of an organization's objectives, industry regulations, and the unique challenges and opportunities presented by AI technologies. This process involves thorough analysis and assessment, as well as collaboration with stakeholders across the organization, from executives and legal teams to data scientists and engineers. By engaging a diverse range of perspectives and expertise, organizations can develop a policy framework that is both tailored to their specific needs and adaptable to the dynamic landscape of AI governance.

In the subsequent sections, we will delve deeper into the key components of building a robust AI corporate compliance policy, exploring best practices and practical considerations for analyzing organizational objectives and industry regulations, developing a tailored policy framework, and ensuring policy adaptability and scalability. By following these guidelines and recommendations, organizations can establish a solid foundation for AI Compliance Excellence, driving responsible innovation and long-term success in the AI-driven business environment.

ALIGNING PRIORITIES: ANALYZING ORGANIZATIONAL OBJECTIVES AND INDUSTRY REGULATIONS FOR EFFECTIVE AI COMPLIANCE

A key step in crafting a robust AI corporate compliance policy is analyzing organizational objectives and industry regulations to ensure that the policy effectively addresses the unique requirements and challenges associated with AI governance. By aligning the compliance policy with the organization's strategic goals and the specific regulatory landscape, businesses can develop a comprehensive and tailored AI governance framework that supports responsible innovation and long-term success.

Understanding organizational objectives is essential for ensuring that the AI compliance policy supports the company's mission, vision, and strategic goals. This process involves engaging with stakeholders across the organization, from executives and business leaders to data scientists and engineers, to identify the desired outcomes and potential benefits of AI-driven initiatives. By aligning the compliance policy with these objectives, organizations can ensure that AI-driven solutions are developed and deployed in a manner that supports their strategic priorities while adhering to legal, regulatory, and ethical requirements.

In addition to considering organizational objectives, it is crucial to analyze industry-specific regulations and guidelines that govern the development, deployment, and management of AI-driven solutions. This process involves staying informed of the latest developments in AI-related laws and regulations, as well as engaging with industry associations, regulatory bodies, and legal experts to gain a comprehensive understanding of the regulatory landscape. By thoroughly analyzing industry regulations, organizations can identify potential compliance gaps, develop appropriate safeguards and controls, and minimize the risk of legal penalties and reputational damage.

Furthermore, organizations must also consider the unique challenges and opportunities presented by AI technologies in their specific industry context. For example, AI-driven solutions in healthcare may require stringent safeguards to protect patient privacy, while AI applications in finance may need to address concerns around algorithmic fairness and transparency. By tailoring the AI compliance policy to address industry-specific requirements and challenges, organizations can effectively mitigate risks and ensure that AI-driven solutions adhere to the highest standards of legal, regulatory, and ethical compliance.

In summary, analyzing organizational objectives and industry regulations is a critical step in developing a robust AI corporate compliance policy. By aligning the policy with the organization's strategic goals and the specific regulatory landscape, businesses can create a comprehensive and tailored AI governance framework that supports responsible innovation and long-term success in the AI-driven business environment.

CUSTOMIZING COMPLIANCE: DEVELOPING A TAILORED AI POLICY FRAMEWORK FOR YOUR ORGANIZATION

Creating a comprehensive AI compliance policy requires a tailored approach that addresses the unique needs, objectives, and challenges of your organization. A customized policy framework not only ensures that AI-driven solutions align with your company's strategic priorities but also demonstrates a commitment to legal, regulatory, and ethical compliance. In this section, we explore the key steps and considerations involved in developing a tailored AI policy framework, empowering your organization to effectively navigate the complexities of AI governance.

First, it is essential to establish a cross-functional team responsible for developing and implementing the AI compliance policy. This team should include representatives from various departments, such as legal, IT, data science, human resources, and business units, to ensure diverse perspectives and expertise are considered. By engaging stakeholders from across the organization, you can create a policy framework that is both comprehensive and relevant to the specific needs and challenges of your company.

Next, conduct a thorough risk assessment to identify potential compliance gaps, vulnerabilities, and areas of improvement in your organization's AI development and deployment processes. This assessment should address various aspects of AI governance, including data privacy and security, algorithmic fairness and transparency, and accountability for AI-driven decisions. By identifying and prioritizing these risks, you can develop targeted strategies and controls to mitigate potential compliance issues.

Once you have a clear understanding of your organization's objectives, industry regulations, and potential risks, begin crafting the policy framework. This framework should provide clear guidelines and expectations for AI development and deployment, addressing key areas such as data management, algorithm design, user privacy, and ethical considerations. Additionally, the framework should outline roles and responsibilities, as well as the processes and procedures for monitoring, reporting, and remediating compliance issues.

To ensure the effectiveness of your tailored policy framework, engage in a continuous improvement process that involves regularly reviewing and updating the policy to address emerging risks, technological advancements, and changes in legal and regulatory requirements. This adaptability is crucial for maintaining a robust and effective AI compliance policy in the dynamic landscape of AI governance.

Developing a tailored AI policy framework is a critical component of crafting a comprehensive and effective AI compliance policy. By engaging stakeholders from across the organization, assessing potential risks, and prioritizing legal, regulatory, and ethical considerations, your organization can establish a solid foundation for AI governance that supports responsible innovation and long-term success in the AI-driven business environment.

FUTURE-PROOFING COMPLIANCE: ENSURING POLICY ADAPTABILITY AND SCALABILITY IN THE AGE OF AI

As the world of AI continues to evolve at a rapid pace, maintaining a robust and effective AI compliance policy requires adaptability and scalability. An adaptable policy allows organizations to respond effectively to changes in legal, regulatory, and ethical requirements, while a scalable policy ensures that AI governance efforts can grow in tandem with the organization's AI-driven initiatives. In this section, we discuss the key strategies for ensuring policy adaptability and scalability, enabling your organization to stay ahead in the dynamic landscape of AI compliance.

To ensure policy adaptability, organizations should establish a process for regularly reviewing and updating their AI compliance policy. This process should involve monitoring developments in AI-related laws and regulations, as well as keeping abreast of emerging trends, technologies, and best practices in AI governance. By staying informed on the latest developments in AI compliance, organizations can proactively adapt their policies to address new challenges and opportunities, minimizing the risk of compliance issues and fostering a culture of continuous improvement.

In addition to monitoring external developments, organizations should also engage in ongoing internal assessments to evaluate the effectiveness of their AI compliance policies. This may involve conducting audits, surveys, and employee feedback sessions to identify areas of improvement and ensure that the policy remains relevant and effective in addressing the organization's unique needs and challenges. By engaging in regular policy reviews and updates, organizations can ensure that their AI governance efforts remain agile and responsive to the ever-changing landscape of AI compliance.

Scalability is another crucial aspect of a robust AI compliance policy. As organizations expand their AI-driven initiatives, the complexity of AI governance increases, necessitating a scalable policy framework that can support growth and manage new risks. To ensure scalability, organizations should consider the following strategies:

1. Develop clear guidelines for AI development and deployment that can be easily adapted to different use cases, industries, and technological advancements.
2. Establish processes and controls that are flexible and modular, allowing for easy integration with new systems, tools, and technologies.
3. Invest in AI-powered compliance tools and solutions that can automate and streamline monitoring, reporting, and remediation processes, enabling organizations to manage growing AI governance demands more efficiently.

By incorporating adaptability and scalability into the AI compliance policy, organizations can effectively navigate the complexities of AI governance and maintain a robust and effective compliance framework in the face of rapid technological advancements and evolving legal, regulatory, and ethical requirements. By embracing this forward-looking approach to AI compliance, organizations can foster responsible innovation, mitigate risks, and drive long-term success in the AI-driven business environment.

FINAL THOUGHTS

As the integration of AI technologies into modern business operations continues to accelerate, the importance of establishing a robust and effective AI compliance policy cannot be overstated. This chapter has explored the essential steps and considerations involved in developing a comprehensive AI compliance policy that supports responsible innovation, mitigates potential risks, and adheres to legal, regulatory, and ethical requirements. By embracing the principles of AI Compliance Excellence, organizations can navigate the complexities of AI governance with confidence, ensuring long-term success in the AI-driven business environment.

Key takeaways from this chapter include:

1. Analyzing organizational objectives and industry regulations is critical for developing a tailored AI compliance

policy that aligns with your organization's strategic goals and addresses industry-specific requirements and challenges.

2. Establishing a cross-functional team, conducting risk assessments, and crafting a comprehensive policy framework are crucial steps in creating a robust and effective AI compliance policy.

3. Ensuring policy adaptability and scalability is vital for maintaining a relevant and effective AI governance framework in the face of rapid technological advancements and evolving legal, regulatory, and ethical requirements.

As organizations continue to harness the transformative potential of AI technologies, a strong commitment to AI compliance will be an essential pillar of success. By adopting a proactive approach to AI governance and continuously refining and adapting their AI compliance policies, organizations can foster a culture of responsibility, drive ethical innovation, and stay ahead in the competitive and rapidly evolving AI landscape.

As we proceed to the subsequent chapters, we will delve into the other crucial aspects of achieving AI Compliance Excellence, including effective employee training, proactive compliance monitoring, leveraging intelligence reports, and continuous improvement. By embracing these strategies and principles, organizations can build a solid foundation for AI Compliance Excellence, positioning themselves for lasting success in the AI-driven business world.

CHAPTER 2

EMPOWERING YOUR WORKFORCE: AN INTRODUCTION TO EFFECTIVE AI COMPLIANCE TRAINING FOR EMPLOYEES

As organizations increasingly rely on AI-driven solutions to streamline operations and drive innovation, it is vital to ensure that employees possess the necessary knowledge and skills to interact responsibly with these technologies. Effective AI compliance training is a critical component of any AI governance strategy, as it enables employees to understand the legal, regulatory, and ethical implications of working with AI and equips them to make informed decisions that minimize risks and promote responsible innovation. In this chapter, we will explore the key principles and strategies for designing and implementing effective AI compliance training programs that empower employees to navigate the complexities of AI compliance with confidence.

AI compliance training should not be considered a one-size-fits-all endeavor. Rather, it should be tailored to the specific needs and objectives of your organization and its workforce. As we delve into the subsequent sections, we will discuss the essential steps involved in designing a comprehensive AI compliance training program, including:

1. Identifying training needs and objectives: Determine the specific knowledge gaps and skill sets that your employees require to ensure responsible AI deployment and usage, and define clear training objectives that align with your organization's overall AI compliance strategy.

2. Designing interactive and engaging training modules: Create training materials that effectively convey complex AI compliance concepts in an accessible and engaging manner, utilizing various formats, such as e-learning modules, workshops, and webinars, to cater to diverse learning preferences and needs.

3. Encouraging a culture of compliance and continuous learning: Foster an organizational culture that values AI compliance and promotes ongoing learning and development, ensuring that employees remain up-to-date on the latest AI governance best practices and requirements.

By investing in effective AI compliance training, organizations can not only minimize potential risks associated with AI usage but also empower their workforce to harness the full potential of AI technologies in an ethical and responsible manner. In the following sections, we will delve deeper into each of these critical aspects of AI compliance training, equipping you with the tools and strategies needed to create a comprehensive and effective training program for your organization.

Charting the Course: Identifying Training Needs and Objectives for AI Compliance

Before embarking on the development of an AI compliance training program, it is crucial to identify the specific training needs and objectives that will best serve your organization and its employees. This process involves assessing the current knowledge and skill levels of your workforce, as well as the unique compliance requirements and challenges associated with your organization's AI-driven initiatives. In this section, we will outline the key steps for identifying training needs and objectives, laying the foundation for an effective AI compliance training program that meets the needs of your organization and empowers your workforce to navigate the complexities of AI compliance with confidence.

1. Conduct a comprehensive needs assessment: Begin by evaluating the current state of AI compliance knowledge and skills within your organization. This may involve surveying employees, conducting interviews, or performing skills assessments to determine areas where additional training is needed. Be sure to consider the varying roles and

responsibilities of employees, as different positions may require different levels of AI compliance expertise.

2. Align training objectives with organizational goals and AI compliance strategy: Ensure that your training objectives align with your organization's overall AI compliance strategy and goals. This may include objectives such as raising awareness of AI compliance risks and regulations, promoting ethical AI practices, or building the skills needed to manage AI-driven projects effectively and responsibly.

3. Consider industry-specific compliance requirements: Depending on your organization's industry, there may be unique compliance requirements and challenges related to AI technologies. Identify these industry-specific concerns and incorporate them into your training objectives, ensuring that your employees are well-equipped to address the unique risks and opportunities associated with AI in your industry.

4. Prioritize training objectives: With a clear understanding of your organization's training needs and objectives, prioritize them based on factors such as the urgency of addressing specific knowledge gaps, the potential impact on AI compliance, and the availability of resources for training development and implementation.

5. Establish a timeline for training delivery: Develop a timeline for delivering the AI compliance training, taking into account factors such as employee availability, the urgency of addressing specific knowledge gaps, and any upcoming AI-related projects or initiatives that may require a well-trained workforce.

By identifying your organization's specific AI compliance training needs and objectives, you can ensure that your training program is tailored to address the unique challenges and requirements of your workforce and industry. This targeted approach will not only maximize the impact and effectiveness of your AI compliance training efforts but also empower your employees to navigate the complexities of AI governance with confidence and competence, driving responsible innovation and long-term success in the AI-driven business landscape.

CAPTIVATING THE LEARNER: DESIGNING INTERACTIVE AND ENGAGING AI COMPLIANCE TRAINING MODULES

Once you have identified your organization's training needs and objectives, the next step is to develop training materials that effectively convey the complex concepts of AI compliance in an accessible and engaging manner. By designing interactive and engaging training modules, you can increase the likelihood of employees retaining and applying the knowledge they acquire, ultimately fostering a culture of responsible AI usage and compliance within your organization. In this section, we will discuss the key principles and strategies for creating captivating AI compliance training modules that inspire active learning and long-term knowledge retention.

1. Utilize a variety of training formats: Cater to diverse learning preferences and needs by incorporating a mix of training formats, such as e-learning modules, workshops, webinars, and even role-play scenarios. This variety will not only help to maintain employee engagement but also ensure that the training content is accessible and digestible for all learners.

2. Employ real-world examples and case studies: Make complex AI compliance concepts more relatable and under-standable by incorporating real-world examples and case studies from your organization or industry. This approach will help employees see the direct relevance and applicability of the training material to their daily work.

3. Foster interactivity and collaboration: Encourage active participation and collaboration among employees by incor-porating interactive elements, such as group discussions, problem-solving activities, and hands-on exercises. These collaborative learning experiences can promote a deeper understanding of AI compliance concepts and help to build a supportive learning environment.

4. Leverage multimedia elements: Enhance the visual appeal and engagement of your training modules by incorporating multimedia elements, such as images, videos, and infograph-ics. These visual aids can help to break up text-heavy content and provide alternative ways for learners to absorb information.

5. Incorporate assessments and feedback opportunities: Embed regular assessments and quizzes throughout the

training modules to gauge employee comprehension and retention of key concepts. Provide timely feedback to help learners identify areas for improvement and track their progress throughout the training program.

6. Adapt training materials to different skill levels: Recognize that employees may possess varying levels of AI compliance knowledge and experience. Develop training materials that cater to different skill levels, offering more advanced content for those with prior experience and foundational material for those new to AI compliance.

By designing interactive and engaging AI compliance training modules, you can create a captivating learning experience that motivates employees to actively engage with the material and apply their newfound knowledge in their daily work. In turn, this investment in effective training will promote a culture of responsible AI usage and compliance, safeguarding your organization from potential risks and ensuring long-term success in the AI-driven business landscape.

FOSTERING A CULTURE OF EXCELLENCE: ENCOURAGING COMPLIANCE AND CONTINUOUS LEARNING IN AI

A well-designed AI compliance training program is only as effective as the organizational culture that supports it. To ensure long-term success in AI compliance, it is essential to

foster a culture that values compliance and promotes continuous learning and development. This will enable employees
to stay up-to-date on the latest AI governance best practices
and requirements, while also cultivating a shared sense of
responsibility for the ethical and compliant use of AI technologies. In this section, we will explore strategies for
encouraging a culture of compliance and continuous
learning in your organization.

1. Set the tone from the top: Leadership plays a critical role
in establishing a culture of compliance and continuous
learning. Ensure that senior leaders actively promote the
importance of AI compliance, model responsible AI practices, and provide ongoing support for employee training
and development initiatives.
2. Establish clear expectations and accountability: Communicate the organization's commitment to AI compliance and
establish clear expectations for employees at all levels. This
may involve setting performance goals related to AI compliance, incorporating compliance objectives into performance
evaluations, or implementing a system for reporting and
addressing potential compliance concerns.
3. Recognize and reward compliance excellence:
Encourage employee engagement in AI compliance initiatives by recognizing and rewarding those who demonstrate
a strong commitment to compliance and continuous learning. This may include offering public recognition,
providing professional development opportunities, or

implementing incentive programs tied to compliance performance.

4. Provide ongoing training and development opportunities: Regularly update and expand your AI compliance training program to address emerging trends, regulations, and best practices. Offer ongoing learning opportunities, such as workshops, webinars, or peer-to-peer mentoring programs, to encourage employees to continuously develop their AI compliance knowledge and skills.

5. Create a supportive learning environment: Foster an open and supportive learning environment where employees feel comfortable discussing AI compliance challenges and sharing best practices. Encourage open communication and collaboration across departments, and provide employees with the resources and support they need to navigate AI compliance complexities with confidence.

6. Measure and track progress: Regularly assess the effectiveness of your AI compliance training program and the overall compliance culture within your organization. Use performance metrics, employee feedback, and compliance incident data to identify areas for improvement and track progress toward your AI compliance goals.

By actively fostering a culture of compliance and continuous learning, your organization can ensure that employees remain informed and engaged in AI compliance initiatives. This investment in creating a supportive and proactive compliance culture will not only minimize potential risks associated with AI usage but also empower your workforce to harness the full potential of AI technologies in an ethical and responsible manner, driving long-term success in the AI-driven business landscape.

GAUGING SUCCESS: ASSESSING AND MEASURING AI COMPLIANCE TRAINING EFFECTIVENESS

To ensure the ongoing success and impact of your AI compliance training program, it is essential to regularly assess and measure its effectiveness. By evaluating the extent to which your training program achieves its objectives, you can identify areas for improvement, optimize the training content, and demonstrate the return on investment in your AI compliance initiatives. In this section, we will discuss key strategies and best practices for assessing and measuring the effectiveness of your AI compliance training program.

1. Define success criteria and performance metrics: Begin by establishing clear success criteria and performance metrics that align with your organization's AI compliance training objectives. These may include knowledge retention rates, improvements in employee performance, reductions in compliance incidents, or increased employee engagement in AI compliance initiatives.

2. Leverage pre- and post-training assessments: Administer assessments before and after the training to measure employees' knowledge and skills in AI compliance. By

comparing pre- and post-training assessment results, you can gauge the effectiveness of the training in improving employee understanding and competence in AI compliance.

3. Collect qualitative feedback: Solicit feedback from employees who participate in the training program through surveys, interviews, or focus groups. This qualitative feedback can provide valuable insights into the strengths and weaknesses of your training content, as well as areas for improvement.

4. Observe on-the-job performance: Monitor employees' on-the-job performance to assess the extent to which they are applying the AI compliance knowledge and skills acquired during the training. This may involve observing employees as they work, reviewing project outcomes, or tracking compliance incidents and violations.

5. Analyze training completion and engagement data: Examine data related to training completion rates, time spent on training modules, and employee engagement with the training content. This information can help you identify potential issues with the accessibility or relevance of your training materials and inform decisions on how to optimize the program.

6. Calculate return on investment (ROI): Assess the financial impact of your AI compliance training program by calculating the return on investment. This may involve comparing the costs associated with the training program to the benefits achieved, such as reduced compliance incidents,

improved employee performance, or increased innovation in AI-driven projects.

7. Conduct ongoing evaluations and improvements: Regularly assess and measure the effectiveness of your AI compliance training program to ensure that it remains relevant, engaging, and impactful. Continuously update and refine the training content based on your evaluation findings, emerging AI compliance trends, and feedback from employees.

By systematically assessing and measuring the effectiveness of your AI compliance training program, you can optimize its impact and ensure that your organization remains well-equipped to navigate the complexities of AI compliance. This proactive approach to training evaluation and improvement will not only safeguard your organization from potential risks but also empower your workforce to drive responsible innovation and long-term success in the AI-driven business landscape.

FINAL THOUGHTS

As we conclude this chapter on AI compliance training, it is evident that investing in effective and engaging training programs is crucial for organizations navigating the ever-evolving AI landscape. By implementing a robust AI compliance training program, businesses can safeguard against potential risks and harness the full potential of AI technologies in a responsible and ethical manner. This chapter has explored various aspects of creating a successful AI compliance training program, from identifying training needs and objectives to designing interactive modules and fostering a culture of continuous learning.

Moreover, we have underscored the importance of assessing and measuring the effectiveness of your training program. By continuously evaluating its impact and refining its content, your organization can ensure that employees remain well-equipped to navigate the complexities of AI compliance. This commitment to AI compliance training excellence will not only minimize potential risks associated with AI usage but also empower your workforce to drive responsible innovation and long-term success in the AI-driven business landscape.

In the subsequent chapters, we will delve into other vital aspects of achieving AI compliance excellence, including proactive compliance monitoring, leveraging intelligence reports, and adapting to the evolving regulatory environment. As you progress through the remainder of this book, we hope you will find valuable insights and practical guidance to help your organization thrive in the age of AI by embracing a comprehensive and proactive approach to AI compliance.

CHAPTER 3

STAYING AHEAD OF THE CURVE: AN INTRODUCTION TO PROACTIVE AI COMPLIANCE MONITORING AND CHECK-INS

IN AN INCREASINGLY COMPLEX AI-DRIVEN BUSINESS landscape, organizations must adopt a proactive approach to AI compliance monitoring and check-ins. By regularly reviewing and assessing the compliance status of AI systems, businesses can quickly identify potential issues, mitigate risks, and maintain a strong compliance posture. In this chapter, we will discuss the importance of proactive AI compliance monitoring and check-ins, as well as strategies and best practices for implementing an effective monitoring program within your organization.

A proactive AI compliance monitoring program involves the use of tools, processes, and systems to continuously evaluate the adherence of AI applications to established compliance policies, regulations, and ethical guidelines. These monitoring efforts should be complemented by regular check-ins with stakeholders, such as AI developers, compliance officers, and business leaders, to ensure ongoing alignment with compliance objectives and to address any emerging concerns.

By implementing proactive AI compliance monitoring and check-ins, organizations can benefit from:

1. Early identification of compliance gaps and potential violations, enabling timely remediation and risk mitigation.
2. Improved transparency and trust in AI systems, as stakeholders can clearly see the steps taken to ensure compliance.
3. Enhanced agility in responding to changes in the regulatory landscape or business requirements, as monitoring efforts can quickly identify areas that require updates or modifications.
4. Streamlined reporting and decision-making, as AI compliance monitoring data can provide valuable insights to inform business strategies and regulatory reporting.
5. Strengthened reputation and relationships with regulators, customers, and partners, who will appreciate the organization's commitment to responsible and compliant AI practices.

In the following sections, we will explore various aspects of proactive AI compliance monitoring and check-ins, including the implementation of AI-powered monitoring and analysis tools, identification of compliance gaps, and streamlining of reporting and remediation processes. By the end of this chapter, you will be equipped with the knowledge and tools to develop a robust AI compliance monitoring program that ensures your organization stays ahead of the curve in the rapidly evolving world of AI.

Harnessing Technology: Implementing AI-Powered Monitoring and Analysis Tools

To effectively navigate the intricacies of AI compliance, organizations must leverage AI-powered monitoring and analysis tools that facilitate the detection and management of compliance risks. These tools can streamline the compliance monitoring process, provide actionable insights, and ultimately contribute to a more robust AI compliance strategy. In this section, we will discuss various AI-powered monitoring and analysis tools and their role in enhancing your organization's AI compliance posture.

1. AI-based data governance solutions: Data governance plays a critical role in ensuring compliance with privacy regulations, security standards, and ethical guidelines. AI-based data governance tools can help organizations automate data classification, data lineage tracking, and data quality management, enabling more effective oversight and control of AI systems' data usage.

2. Natural language processing (NLP) tools: NLP-powered solutions can analyze textual data from various sources, such as regulations, policies, and contracts, to identify relevant

compliance requirements and potential risks. By automating the analysis of complex legal documents, NLP tools can reduce the time and effort required to stay up-to-date with regulatory changes and ensure AI systems comply with applicable laws.

3. Anomaly detection and predictive analytics: AI-powered anomaly detection algorithms can analyze patterns in AI system behavior to identify deviations from expected performance or compliance standards. By leveraging predictive analytics, organizations can anticipate potential compliance risks before they materialize, allowing for proactive remediation measures.

4. Machine learning-driven risk assessment: Machine learning techniques can be employed to assess and prioritize compliance risks associated with AI systems. By training models on historical data, organizations can gain insights into the likelihood and impact of potential compliance issues, enabling more informed decision-making and resource allocation.

5. Automated compliance reporting: AI-powered tools can streamline the compliance reporting process by automating data collection, analysis, and visualization. These tools can help organizations generate accurate, timely, and consistent reports for internal stakeholders and regulatory authorities, reducing the risk of manual errors and improving overall transparency.

6. Continuous monitoring and alerting: By implementing continuous monitoring solutions, organizations can track AI

systems' compliance status in real-time, enabling the rapid detection of potential violations or risks. AI-powered alerting mechanisms can notify relevant stakeholders of emerging issues, ensuring timely response and remediation.

When selecting and implementing AI-powered monitoring and analysis tools, organizations should consider factors such as integration capabilities, scalability, customization options, and ease of use. By harnessing the power of AI to enhance compliance monitoring efforts, businesses can more effectively identify, assess, and manage compliance risks, fostering a culture of accountability and responsibility in the era of AI-driven innovation.

Closing the Gap: Identifying Compliance Gaps and Potential Violations in AI Systems

Effectively managing AI compliance requires organizations to be vigilant in identifying compliance gaps and potential violations within their AI systems. Timely detection and remediation of these issues are crucial for mitigating risks and maintaining a strong compliance posture. In this section, we will discuss strategies for identifying compliance gaps and potential violations, and the importance of addressing these concerns proactively.

1. Conduct regular audits and assessments: Periodic audits

and assessments of AI systems can help organizations identify compliance gaps and potential violations. These evaluations should encompass both technical aspects, such as data
handling, algorithmic transparency, and security measures,
and procedural elements, including policy adherence,
employee training, and incident reporting processes. By
conducting regular audits, organizations can ensure that
their AI systems are operating in line with regulatory
requirements and internal policies.

2. Monitor AI system performance and outputs: Continuously monitoring the performance and outputs of AI
systems can reveal instances of biased decision-making, data
breaches, or other potential violations. By analyzing patterns
in AI-generated results, organizations can detect anomalies
that may signal compliance issues and take corrective action
as needed.

3. Foster a culture of compliance and open communication:
Encouraging a culture of compliance and open communication within the organization can facilitate the identification
of compliance gaps and potential violations. By empowering
employees to report concerns and fostering a safe environment for raising issues, organizations can tap into their
workforce's collective knowledge and experience to identify
and address compliance concerns more effectively.

4. Leverage AI-powered compliance tools: As discussed in
the previous section, AI-powered monitoring and analysis
tools can help organizations identify compliance gaps and
potential violations in their AI systems. By implementing

these tools, businesses can automate the detection and assessment of compliance risks, enabling more efficient and proactive risk management.

5. Collaborate with external experts and regulatory bodies: Partnering with external experts, such as consultants, legal advisors, and industry associations, can provide valuable insights into potential compliance risks and best practices for addressing them. Regular engagement with regulatory bodies can also help organizations stay abreast of emerging requirements and guidelines, ensuring that their AI systems remain compliant with evolving standards.

By proactively identifying and addressing compliance gaps and potential violations, organizations can minimize the risks associated with AI systems and maintain a strong compliance posture. In the next section, we will explore strategies for streamlining reporting and remediation processes to further enhance your organization's AI compliance efforts.

STREAMLINING THE PATH TO COMPLIANCE: OPTIMIZING REPORTING AND REMEDIATION PROCESSES IN AI SYSTEMS

In the fast-paced world of AI-driven innovation, organizations must be able to quickly and efficiently report and remediate compliance issues to maintain a strong compliance posture. Streamlined reporting and remediation

processes not only minimize the impact of compliance violations but also demonstrate the organization's commitment to
maintaining the highest ethical standards. In this section, we
will discuss strategies for optimizing reporting and remediation processes within your organization.

1. Establish clear reporting channels and protocols: To facilitate efficient reporting of compliance issues, organizations
should establish clear and accessible reporting channels and
protocols. These channels may include dedicated hotlines,
email addresses, or web portals for employees to report
concerns. Providing guidelines on the types of information
to include in a report and the expected response time can
help improve the quality and timeliness of incident
reporting.
2. Develop a centralized incident management system:
Implementing a centralized incident management system
can help organizations track, prioritize, and address compliance issues more effectively. This system should enable
stakeholders to log incidents, assign responsibility for investigation and remediation, and monitor progress towards resolution. Centralizing incident management can also provide
valuable data for trend analysis and continuous improvement efforts.
3. Implement automated workflows and escalation procedures: Automated workflows can streamline the reporting
and remediation process by reducing manual tasks and
ensuring a timely response to compliance incidents. By

incorporating escalation procedures, organizations can ensure that more severe incidents receive the appropriate level of attention from senior management or external stakeholders, such as regulatory authorities.

4. Foster cross-functional collaboration: Addressing compliance issues often requires input from multiple departments, including legal, IT, human resources, and data privacy teams. By fostering cross-functional collaboration, organizations can ensure a holistic approach to incident investigation and remediation, leveraging the expertise of various stakeholders to address complex compliance challenges.

5. Train employees on reporting and remediation processes: Providing employees with training on reporting and remediation processes can enhance their ability to identify, report, and address compliance issues effectively. This training should cover topics such as the organization's expectations for reporting, available reporting channels, and the steps involved in the remediation process.

6. Continuously evaluate and improve processes: Regularly reviewing and refining reporting and remediation processes can help organizations identify inefficiencies and areas for improvement. By incorporating feedback from employees, lessons learned from past incidents, and industry best practices, organizations can continuously enhance their compliance management capabilities.

By streamlining reporting and remediation processes, organizations can more effectively address compliance issues, reduce the risk of violations, and demonstrate their commitment to maintaining the highest standards of AI compliance. In the following sections, we will explore additional strategies for achieving AI compliance excellence, including leveraging intelligence reports, embracing continuous improvement, and adapting to emerging trends and technologies.

Final Thoughts

As we conclude this chapter, it is crucial to recognize the importance of proactive AI compliance monitoring and the implementation of streamlined reporting and remediation processes in fostering a strong compliance posture. Organizations that invest in these areas are better equipped to identify, address, and prevent compliance issues, minimizing the risks associated with AI-driven innovation while maximizing the benefits it offers.

To recap the key takeaways from this chapter:

1. Implement AI-powered monitoring and analysis tools to detect compliance gaps and potential violations in real-time, enabling swift and effective responses to emerging risks.
2. Establish clear reporting channels and protocols to facilitate the timely and accurate reporting of compliance incidents, ensuring that issues are promptly addressed and resolved.
3. Develop a centralized incident management system to

efficiently track, prioritize, and remediate compliance issues, fostering a holistic approach to compliance management.

4. Foster cross-functional collaboration and train employees on reporting and remediation processes, empowering your workforce to proactively contribute to your organization's AI compliance efforts.

5. Continuously evaluate and improve your organization's monitoring, reporting, and remediation processes, incorporating lessons learned, feedback, and industry best practices to drive continuous improvement.

By integrating these strategies into your AI compliance program, your organization will be better positioned to navigate the complex landscape of AI regulations and guidelines, ensuring that your AI systems operate in a manner that is both ethical and compliant. In the next chapter, we will explore the role of intelligence reports in informing your AI compliance efforts, providing insights into industry trends, regulatory updates, and best practices for managing AI risks.

CHAPTER 4

HARNESSING THE POWER OF INTELLIGENCE: MAXIMIZING AI COMPLIANCE THROUGH INDUSTRY INSIGHTS AND REGULATORY UPDATES

IN THE RAPIDLY EVOLVING WORLD OF AI, STAYING INFORMED on the latest industry trends, regulatory developments, and best practices is essential for maintaining a robust and effective AI compliance program. Intelligence reports offer valuable insights that can inform your organization's AI compliance strategy, enabling you to stay ahead of the curve and adapt to the changing landscape.

By tapping into the wealth of knowledge contained in intelligence reports, your organization can gain a deeper understanding of emerging AI technologies, their applications, and the potential compliance challenges they pose. This allows you to proactively address these risks and capitalize on new opportunities. Additionally, staying abreast of changes in the regulatory environment ensures that your AI compliance program remains up-to-date and in line with evolving legal requirements. This not only helps you avoid potential penalties but also demonstrates your commitment to maintaining the highest ethical standards in your AI initiatives.

Furthermore, intelligence reports can provide insights into best practices adopted by industry leaders, enabling you to benchmark your compliance efforts against those of your peers and identify areas for improvement. By learning from the successes and failures of other organizations, you can refine your own AI compliance strategies and drive continuous improvement in your program.

To make the most of intelligence reports, it is crucial to establish a system for regularly monitoring and disseminating relevant information throughout your organization. This may involve subscribing to industry newsletters, attending webinars and conferences, or partnering with external consultants who specialize in AI compliance. Encouraging cross-functional collaboration can also help ensure that insights from intelligence reports are integrated into your organization's decision-making processes, fostering a culture of compliance that extends across all levels and functions.

In summary, leveraging intelligence reports is a powerful tool for achieving AI compliance excellence, as it empowers your organization to stay informed, adapt to change, and continuously refine your compliance program. In the following sections, we will discuss additional strategies for maintaining a strong AI compliance posture, including embracing continuous improvement, fostering a culture of compliance, and collaborating with industry peers and regulatory bodies.

NAVIGATING THE COMPLEX LANDSCAPE: STAYING INFORMED ON LEGAL AND CORPORATE COMPLIANCE CONCERNS

In today's dynamic and complex regulatory environment, keeping up with legal and corporate compliance concerns is more critical than ever, especially for organizations incorporating AI-driven innovation. Staying informed on these matters not only helps your organization maintain a strong compliance posture but also enables you to proactively address potential issues before they escalate, minimizing risks and enhancing your reputation as a responsible corporate citizen.

One effective strategy for staying informed is to establish a dedicated compliance team. Building a team of compliance experts, including legal professionals and AI specialists, can help ensure that your organization remains updated on the latest developments in AI regulations, guidelines, and best practices. This team can also be responsible for monitoring and evaluating the effectiveness of your AI compliance program and recommending improvements as needed.

Another approach is to regularly monitor regulatory updates. Reviewing information from regulatory bodies and government agencies, such as the European Union's GDPR, the U.S. Federal Trade Commission, and other relevant organizations, will help you stay current on new rules and guidelines that may impact your AI compliance efforts. Moreover, participating in industry associations, attending conferences, and subscribing to relevant newsletters can provide valuable insights into the latest compliance trends and best practices.

Finally, fostering a culture of compliance throughout your organization is crucial. Encourage open communication and collaboration between different departments, ensuring that all employees understand the importance of compliance and their role in maintaining a strong compliance posture. Provide regular training and updates on legal and corporate compliance concerns to empower your workforce with the knowledge and skills needed to effectively navigate the ever-evolving landscape of AI regulations and guidelines.

EMBRACING CHANGE: ADAPTING TO NEW DEVELOPMENTS IN THE AI WORLD

The world of AI is constantly evolving, with new technologies, applications, and use cases emerging at an unprecedented pace. To remain competitive and ensure compliance in this fast-paced environment, organizations must be agile and adaptable, embracing change and incorporating new developments into their AI strategies and compliance programs.

One key aspect of adapting to new developments in the AI world is staying informed about cutting-edge technologies and innovations. By closely monitoring industry news, attending conferences, and engaging in professional networks, you can gain insights into the latest advancements and their potential implications for your organization's AI initiatives. This knowledge can help you identify opportunities for leveraging new AI solutions while also anticipating and addressing any compliance challenges that may arise.

As new developments emerge, it is crucial to reassess and adjust your AI compliance program accordingly. This may involve updating policies and procedures, refining risk assessment processes, and implementing new controls and safeguards to ensure that your organization remains in compliance with relevant regulations and industry standards. It is also essential to provide ongoing training and education for your employees, equipping them with the knowledge and skills needed to navigate the shifting landscape of AI compliance effectively.

In addition to adapting your compliance program, embracing new developments in the AI world may require adjustments to your organization's broader strategic goals and objectives. By aligning your AI strategy with emerging trends and technologies, you can capitalize on new opportunities, drive innovation, and maintain a competitive edge in the market. This alignment may involve reevaluating your organization's AI investments, partnerships, and talent acquisition strategies to ensure that you are well-positioned to thrive in the ever-evolving AI landscape.

In summary, adapting to new developments in the AI world is critical for maintaining AI compliance excellence and staying ahead of the curve. By staying informed, regularly updating your compliance program, and aligning your AI strategy with emerging trends, your organization can effectively navigate the challenges and opportunities presented by the rapidly evolving world of AI.

TURNING INSIGHTS INTO ACTION: DRIVING POLICY AND TRAINING IMPROVEMENTS THROUGH DATA-DRIVEN INSIGHTS

In the rapidly evolving world of AI, harnessing the power of data-driven insights is essential for organizations seeking to optimize their AI compliance programs and training initiatives. By leveraging the wealth of information generated through compliance monitoring, risk assessments, and employee performance metrics, organizations can identify opportunities for improvement, make informed decisions, and drive continuous growth in AI compliance excellence.

One crucial area where insights can be utilized to drive improvements is in the development and refinement of AI compliance policies. By analyzing data from various sources, such as internal audits, regulatory inspections, and incident reports, organizations can identify patterns and trends that may indicate gaps or vulnerabilities in their existing policies.

This information can then be used to inform policy updates, ensuring that compliance efforts remain aligned with the latest regulatory requirements and industry best practices.

Similarly, insights can be employed to enhance AI compliance training programs. By evaluating the effectiveness of training initiatives through metrics such as employee performance, knowledge retention, and engagement levels, organizations can pinpoint areas for improvement and tailor their training content and delivery methods accordingly. For example, if data reveals that employees are struggling to understand a particular aspect of AI compliance, training modules can be updated to provide clearer explanations, additional examples, or more interactive learning experiences.

Moreover, insights can be used to inform the development of targeted training programs for specific employee groups or departments. By analyzing data on compliance risks and incidents, organizations can identify areas where specialized training may be needed to address unique challenges or knowledge gaps. Customized training programs can then be created to provide the necessary support and education for these employees, ultimately improving overall compliance performance.

The effective utilization of data-driven insights can play a pivotal role in driving policy and training improvements for AI compliance. By identifying trends, patterns, and opportunities for growth, organizations can continuously refine their compliance efforts, ensuring that they remain agile, adaptable, and prepared to meet the ever-changing demands of the AI landscape.

FINAL THOUGHTS

The pursuit of AI compliance excellence is an ongoing journey, requiring organizations to remain agile, adaptable, and proactive in their efforts. By leveraging expert guidance, conducting routine compliance check-ins and monitoring, staying abreast of industry trends and regulatory updates, and continually refining policies and training programs, organizations can effectively navigate the complex landscape of AI compliance and minimize associated risks.

The key to success in this journey lies in harnessing the power of data-driven insights to inform decision-making and drive continuous improvement. By systematically gathering, analyzing, and acting upon the wealth of information generated through compliance activities and employee performance metrics, organizations can identify opportunities for growth and optimization, ultimately enhancing the effectiveness and resilience of their AI compliance programs.

As AI continues to transform industries and reshape the global business landscape, the importance of AI compliance excellence cannot be overstated. Organizations that prioritize compliance and embrace the principles outlined in this chapter will be well-positioned to navigate the challenges and opportunities presented by AI, fostering a culture of innovation, accountability, and ethical responsibility that ensures long-term success and sustainability.

As we move forward into the dynamic world of AI, let us embrace the power of insights and the principles of AI compliance excellence to guide our path, ensuring that we harness the full potential of AI while upholding the highest standards of ethical and legal responsibility.

CHAPTER 5

EMBRACING CHANGE AND GROWTH: AN INTRODUCTION TO CONTINUOUS IMPROVEMENT AND ADAPTATION IN AI COMPLIANCE

THE WORLD OF AI IS CHARACTERIZED BY RAPID INNOVATION and ever-evolving technologies, making it crucial for organizations to adopt a mindset of continuous improvement and adaptation when it comes to AI compliance. As new developments, regulatory changes, and ethical considerations emerge, organizations must be prepared to respond proactively, refining their compliance policies, training programs, and monitoring strategies to ensure ongoing alignment with the latest best practices and industry standards.

In this section, we will explore the importance of embracing change and fostering a culture of continuous improvement in the realm of AI compliance. We will discuss the key elements of a resilient and adaptable AI compliance program and offer guidance on how organizations can collaborate with industry peers, regulatory bodies, and other stakeholders to stay informed and responsive to emerging trends and challenges. By prioritizing continuous improvement and adaptation, organizations can ensure that their AI compliance efforts remain effective, relevant, and aligned with their long-term strategic objectives.

NAVIGATING THE DYNAMIC LANDSCAPE: EMBRACING CHANGE AND EVOLVING COMPLIANCE NEEDS

The rapidly changing landscape of AI technology requires organizations to be agile and adaptable in their compliance efforts. Embracing change and evolving compliance needs is essential to ensure that AI-driven processes and systems adhere to the latest regulatory requirements, ethical standards, and industry best practices. By fostering a culture that is open to change and prioritizes learning, organizations can effectively navigate the uncertainties and challenges that come with AI adoption.

To embrace change and evolving compliance needs, organizations must stay informed about technological advancements, regulatory updates, and shifts in industry expectations. Regular reviews and updates of compliance policies and training programs are crucial to ensure that they remain relevant and effective. It is important to involve all levels of the organization in this process, from senior leadership to frontline employees, as collective understanding and commitment to change is essential for successful implementation.

Additionally, organizations should establish feedback mechanisms that enable continuous learning from compliance-related incidents and experiences. By systematically collecting and analyzing data on compliance performance and emerging risks, organizations can identify areas for improvement and implement targeted strategies to enhance their AI compliance efforts.

In summary, embracing change and evolving compliance needs is critical for organizations to stay ahead of the curve in the fast-paced world of AI. By fostering a culture of learning, adaptability, and continuous improvement, organizations can ensure that their AI compliance programs remain effective and aligned with the latest developments in technology, regulation, and ethical standards.

CULTIVATING SUCCESS: FOSTERING A MINDSET OF CONTINUOUS IMPROVEMENT IN AI COMPLIANCE

The key to maintaining a successful AI compliance program lies in fostering a mindset of continuous improvement within the organization. By encouraging employees at all levels to actively seek ways to enhance their understanding of AI compliance and contribute to the ongoing refinement of policies, training programs, and monitoring strategies, organizations can drive sustainable growth and adapt more effectively to the ever-changing AI landscape.

To foster a mindset of continuous improvement, organizations should prioritize open communication and collaboration across departments and teams. This involves creating an environment where employees feel comfortable sharing their insights, experiences, and suggestions for improvement, and where these contributions are valued and acted upon. Regular meetings, workshops, and training sessions can be organized to facilitate the exchange of ideas and promote a culture of continuous learning.

In addition to encouraging employee engagement, organizations must also invest in the necessary tools, resources, and technologies that support continuous improvement in AI compliance. This may include AI-powered monitoring and analysis systems, up-to-date training materials, and access to relevant industry intelligence and research. By providing employees with the resources they need to stay informed and upskill, organizations can empower them to play an active role in driving AI compliance excellence.

Finally, organizations should establish performance metrics and benchmarks to measure the effectiveness of their AI compliance efforts and identify areas for improvement. By regularly reviewing and analyzing these metrics, organizations can make data-driven decisions on where to focus their improvement initiatives and ensure that their AI compliance program remains aligned with their strategic objectives.

Fostering a mindset of continuous improvement is critical to achieving and maintaining AI compliance excellence. By cultivating a culture of open communication, collaboration, and ongoing learning, organizations can ensure that their AI compliance efforts remain relevant, effective, and responsive to the dynamic world of AI technology.

BUILDING BRIDGES: COLLABORATING WITH INDUSTRY PEERS AND REGULATORY BODIES FOR AI COMPLIANCE EXCELLENCE

In the rapidly evolving world of AI, collaboration is crucial to staying informed and adapting to the latest compliance requirements, industry best practices, and technological advancements. By actively engaging with industry peers and regulatory bodies, organizations can not only enhance their own AI compliance programs but also contribute to the broader development of robust, ethical, and effective AI practices across the entire sector.

Collaborating with industry peers enables organizations to learn from each other's experiences, challenges, and successes in AI compliance. By participating in industry forums, conferences, and workshops, organizations can exchange valuable insights and knowledge, discuss emerging trends and issues, and identify potential areas for collaboration. Joint initiatives, such as the development of shared standards or the pooling of resources for compliance-related research, can lead to more effective and efficient compliance strategies for all participants.

Engaging with regulatory bodies is another essential component of a successful AI compliance strategy. By maintaining open lines of communication with regulators and participating in the development of new guidelines and regulations, organizations can better understand the intentions and expectations of regulatory bodies, as well as contribute to shaping the future direction of AI compliance. Furthermore, proactively seeking guidance from regulators on specific compliance challenges can help organizations address potential issues before they escalate, minimizing the risk of non-compliance and associated penalties.

In addition to the benefits of collaboration, working closely with industry peers and regulatory bodies also demonstrates an organization's commitment to ethical and responsible AI practices. This can enhance the organization's reputation among customers, investors, and other stakeholders, and position it as a leader in AI compliance excellence.

Collaborating with industry peers and regulatory bodies is a critical aspect of achieving and maintaining AI compliance excellence. By engaging in open dialogue, sharing knowledge, and working together to develop robust compliance strategies, organizations can stay ahead of the curve and contribute to the advancement of ethical, responsible, and effective AI practices across the entire industry.

HARNESSING COLLECTIVE WISDOM: INCORPORATING FEEDBACK FROM EMPLOYEES AND STAKEHOLDERS FOR AI COMPLIANCE EXCELLENCE

In the pursuit of AI compliance excellence, it is essential to recognize the value of feedback from both employees and stakeholders. By actively seeking and incorporating their insights, organizations can strengthen their AI compliance programs and create a culture that promotes accountability, transparency, and continuous improvement.

Employees are on the frontlines of AI implementation, and their firsthand experience with AI systems and processes is invaluable for identifying areas of improvement and potential risks. Encourage open communication by creating channels for employees to share their insights, concerns, and suggestions related to AI compliance. This can include regular town hall meetings, anonymous reporting systems, or dedicated feedback platforms. Additionally, consider incorporating AI compliance into performance evaluations to emphasize its importance and encourage ongoing engagement from employees.

Stakeholders, such as customers, suppliers, investors, and regulators, also offer unique perspectives on an organization's AI compliance program. By soliciting their feedback, organizations can better understand how their AI initiatives impact various aspects of their business, from customer satisfaction to regulatory compliance. Engaging with stakeholders can be done through surveys, focus groups, or ongoing dialogue in forums and committees.

Once feedback has been collected, it is crucial to act on it. Establish a process for reviewing and prioritizing the feedback, and involve relevant teams in developing and implementing action plans. Regularly communicate the progress and outcomes of these initiatives to employees and stakeholders, demonstrating that their input is valued and making them feel more invested in the organization's AI compliance efforts.

By incorporating feedback from employees and stakeholders, organizations can not only address potential compliance risks and shortcomings but also foster a culture that values diverse perspectives and promotes continuous improvement. This collaborative approach to AI compliance helps ensure that organizations remain agile and adaptable in the face of an ever-changing regulatory landscape and positions them for long-term success in the age of AI.

FINAL THOUGHTS

As we conclude this chapter, it is essential to recognize that the journey toward AI compliance excellence is an ongoing process, one that requires dedication, adaptability, and a commitment to continuous improvement. The strategies and best practices discussed in this chapter are designed to help organizations build a strong foundation for their AI compliance programs, but it is crucial to remember that these are just the beginning.

AI technology continues to evolve at a rapid pace, as do the regulatory and ethical considerations surrounding it. To maintain AI compliance excellence, organizations must stay vigilant, agile, and proactive in adapting to these changes. This includes regularly revisiting and refining their compliance policies, training programs, monitoring efforts, and stakeholder engagement initiatives.

A culture that embraces change and fosters a mindset of continuous improvement is vital for navigating the dynamic landscape of AI compliance. By empowering employees and stakeholders to contribute their insights and perspectives, organizations can create an environment where AI compliance is everyone's responsibility and a shared goal.

In summary, the journey toward AI compliance excellence is one of constant evolution and collaboration. By committing to continuous improvement and adaptation, organizations can not only minimize risks and ensure regulatory compliance but also unlock the full potential of AI to drive innovation, efficiency, and growth. As you progress through the remaining chapters of this book, keep this mindset at the forefront and remember that the pursuit of AI compliance excellence is an ongoing, collaborative effort that will empower your organization to thrive in the age of AI.

CHAPTER 6

NAVIGATING AI COMPLIANCE IN MERGERS AND ACQUISITIONS

IN TODAY'S RAPIDLY EVOLVING BUSINESS LANDSCAPE, MERGERS and acquisitions (M&A) are increasingly common as organizations seek to expand their operations, acquire new technologies, or strengthen their market position. One critical aspect of any M&A process that often goes overlooked is the seamless integration and management of AI systems, particularly from a compliance perspective. As AI becomes more ingrained in various industries and business operations, ensuring AI compliance during and after M&A transactions is vital to avoid potential risks, legal liabilities, and reputational harm.

In this chapter, we will delve into the unique challenges and opportunities that arise in the context of M&A as they relate to AI compliance. We will explore the importance of conducting thorough due diligence to identify and address

AI compliance issues, as well as the best practices for effectively integrating AI policies and practices post-acquisition. Additionally, we will discuss strategies for managing the complex compliance landscape that often emerges when two or more organizations with differing AI systems, policies, and regulations join forces.

By understanding the nuances of AI compliance in M&A scenarios and adopting a proactive approach, organizations can navigate the complexities of these transactions while minimizing potential risks and ensuring a smooth transition. This chapter aims to equip you with the knowledge and tools necessary to confidently tackle AI compliance challenges in the context of mergers and acquisitions, ultimately contributing to the overall success of your organization's growth and expansion strategies.

DUE DILIGENCE IN AI COMPLIANCE DURING M&A PROCESSES: AN ESSENTIAL PRACTICE

Due diligence is a critical component of any merger or acquisition, as it allows organizations to identify potential risks and liabilities before finalizing a transaction. When it comes to AI compliance, conducting thorough due diligence is of paramount importance to ensure that the acquired entity's AI systems, policies, and practices align with the acquiring organization's compliance requirements, legal obligations, and ethical standards.

In the context of AI compliance, due diligence should

involve a comprehensive review of the target organization's AI systems and processes. This includes evaluating the quality and accuracy of their AI algorithms, the fairness and transparency of their decision-making processes, and the robustness of their data privacy and security measures. It is also crucial to assess the target organization's adherence to industry-specific regulations, as well as any international guidelines or best practices that may apply.

During the due diligence process, acquiring organizations should pay close attention to the target entity's AI training programs, monitoring and reporting mechanisms, and incident response plans. Understanding how the target organization addresses AI compliance issues will enable the acquiring company to identify any gaps or inconsistencies that may require attention during the post-acquisition integration phase.

By conducting thorough AI compliance due diligence, organizations can not only minimize potential legal and reputational risks but also gain valuable insights into the target company's AI capabilities, culture, and overall approach to compliance. This information can then be used to inform the integration process, ensuring a smoother transition and ultimately contributing to the long-term success of the merged entity.

Integrating AI Policies and Practices Post-Acquisition: Fostering a Unified Approach

Successfully integrating AI policies and practices following a merger or acquisition is crucial for maintaining compliance and ensuring a seamless transition. This process involves harmonizing the AI systems, standards, and frameworks of the involved organizations to create a consistent and cohesive approach to AI compliance across the newly formed entity.

The first step in integrating AI policies and practices is to conduct a thorough review of both organizations' existing AI compliance frameworks. This enables the identification of potential overlaps, gaps, and discrepancies that may need to be addressed. It is essential to consider various factors, such as industry-specific regulations, international guidelines, and the organizations' unique compliance requirements.

Once the review is complete, the next step is to develop a unified AI compliance policy that encompasses the best practices of both organizations. This policy should be clear, comprehensive, and flexible enough to accommodate future developments in AI technology and regulatory landscapes. In some cases, it may be necessary to establish a cross-functional team consisting of AI experts, legal professionals, and representatives from key business units to ensure that the new policy addresses all relevant concerns and stakeholder interests.

With a unified AI compliance policy in place, the next phase is to align the organizations' AI training programs, monitoring and reporting mechanisms, and remediation processes. This may involve updating training materials, streamlining reporting channels, and creating standardized incident response procedures.

Finally, it is essential to communicate the changes effectively to employees and stakeholders. This can be achieved through training sessions, workshops, and ongoing support to ensure that everyone understands the new policies, procedures, and expectations regarding AI compliance. By fostering a culture of continuous learning and improvement, organizations can successfully integrate their AI policies and practices post-acquisition, creating a stronger, more resilient, and compliant entity.

ADDRESSING COMPLIANCE CHALLENGES IN MERGED ORGANIZATIONS: OVERCOMING OBSTACLES AND ENSURING SUCCESS

The merger of two or more organizations often presents a unique set of AI compliance challenges. As companies combine their systems, policies, and procedures, they must work diligently to ensure that AI compliance remains a top priority. Addressing these challenges is critical to the success of the newly formed entity, and organizations should be prepared to tackle them head-on.

One of the primary challenges in merged organizations

is the harmonization of disparate AI compliance policies, procedures, and training programs. Aligning these elements may require considerable effort and resources, as well as the involvement of key stakeholders from both organizations. It is crucial to establish a unified AI compliance framework that reflects the needs and objectives of the newly formed entity while adhering to all relevant regulatory requirements.

Another challenge is managing the potential cultural differences between the merging organizations, which may impact how employees perceive and approach AI compliance. Encouraging a culture of compliance across the newly formed organization involves open communication, shared values, and a commitment to continuous learning. Providing employees with the necessary training, resources, and support can facilitate a smooth transition and foster a consistent compliance culture.

Additionally, merged organizations must address the issue of data privacy and security. Combining data from multiple sources can introduce new risks, and organizations must take appropriate measures to protect sensitive information while maintaining compliance with relevant data protection regulations. This may involve reviewing and updating data storage and processing policies, implementing robust security measures, and conducting regular audits to ensure ongoing compliance.

Lastly, organizations should be prepared to manage potential regulatory scrutiny during and after the merger process. Ensuring that all AI compliance obligations are met can help prevent legal issues and potential fines, as well as maintain the trust of customers, partners, and other stakeholders.

By proactively addressing these compliance challenges, merged organizations can successfully navigate the complexities of AI compliance and ensure a smooth transition into a unified, compliant, and successful entity.

FINAL THOUGHTS

The process of merging organizations presents unique challenges in terms of AI compliance. However, with a proactive approach and thorough planning, these challenges can be effectively addressed to ensure a smooth transition and continued compliance excellence. By focusing on the harmonization of AI policies and practices, fostering a unified culture of compliance, safeguarding data privacy and security, and managing regulatory scrutiny, merged organizations can successfully navigate the complexities of AI compliance and maintain a strong footing in the rapidly evolving landscape of AI and technology.

As companies continue to embrace AI and its applications, the importance of AI compliance in mergers and acquisitions will only grow. It is essential for organizations to stay informed of new developments, learn from industry best practices, and adapt their strategies to accommodate the evolving regulatory environment. By prioritizing

AI compliance and investing in the right resources, organizations can ensure their long-term success and sustainability in the face of change and disruption. Embracing AI compliance excellence is not just a matter of legal obligation, but a strategic imperative that contributes to an organization's competitive advantage and reputation in the modern business landscape.

CHAPTER 7

NAVIGATING THE COMPLEXITIES OF GLOBAL LEGAL CONSIDERATIONS IN AI COMPLIANCE

IN TODAY'S INCREASINGLY INTERCONNECTED WORLD, businesses are operating on a global scale, and this has significant implications for AI compliance. As organizations expand their operations across borders, they must navigate a complex web of international regulations and guidelines that govern the use of artificial intelligence and related technologies. Understanding and adhering to these legal requirements is vital for businesses to minimize risk, protect their brand reputation, and maintain their competitive advantage.

This chapter will explore the intricacies of global legal considerations in AI compliance, providing a roadmap for organizations seeking to establish a robust compliance program that addresses the unique challenges associated with international operations. We will discuss the importance of understanding and adapting to various international AI regulations and guidelines, as well as the cross-border data privacy and security concerns that must be considered when implementing AI solutions. By the end of this chapter, readers will have a deeper appreciation of the complexities of global legal considerations and will be better equipped to develop and maintain an AI compliance program that accommodates the nuances of operating in a global context.

Navigating International AI Regulations and Guidelines: Achieving Compliance Across Borders

As businesses increasingly adopt AI technologies and expand their global footprint, they must be prepared to navigate the diverse landscape of international AI regulations and guidelines. Different countries and regions have varying legal frameworks and requirements, making compliance a complex task for organizations operating on a global scale. Failure to adhere to these rules can result in significant fines, reputational damage, and even legal action.

To successfully navigate international AI regulations and guidelines, organizations must first invest in research and knowledge acquisition. This involves staying informed of the latest developments in AI laws and regulations across the countries in which they operate. It is essential to be aware of not only the specific legal requirements but also the broader context of each jurisdiction's approach to AI governance, which may include ethical considerations and data protection principles.

Collaboration with local experts and legal counsel is a critical component of navigating international AI regulations. These professionals possess in-depth knowledge of regional laws and can provide valuable guidance on implementing compliant AI solutions. Additionally, businesses should engage in regular communication with local regulators to ensure they are up-to-date with any changes in the regulatory landscape.

Another key aspect of navigating international AI regulations is the development of a flexible and adaptable compliance framework. Given the dynamic nature of AI-related laws and guidelines, it is crucial that organizations establish policies and procedures that can be easily modified to accommodate new requirements. This may involve creating a centralized compliance team that oversees AI compliance efforts across all jurisdictions or adopting a modular approach to policy development that allows for targeted adjustments in response to specific regulatory changes.

By taking a proactive approach to understanding and adapting to international AI regulations and guidelines, organizations can not only minimize their risk exposure but also demonstrate a commitment to responsible AI practices that fosters trust with customers, partners, and regulators alike.

ADAPTING AI COMPLIANCE POLICIES FOR GLOBAL OPERATIONS: STRIKING A BALANCE BETWEEN CONSISTENCY AND FLEXIBILITY

As businesses expand their global operations and incorporate AI technologies, they must strike a delicate balance between maintaining consistency in their AI compliance policies and adapting to the unique regulatory environments of each region in which they operate. A one-size-fits-all approach to AI compliance may not be sufficient, as it can leave organizations vulnerable to non-compliance issues in certain jurisdictions. In this context, it becomes imperative for organizations to develop tailored AI compliance policies that can accommodate the diverse legal landscapes across the globe.

The first step in adapting AI compliance policies for global operations is to establish a strong foundation built on a thorough understanding of the core principles and best practices for AI compliance. This includes identifying common ethical considerations, data protection requirements, and transparency obligations that are likely to be relevant across multiple jurisdictions. By building upon this foundation, organizations can create a baseline policy that serves as a starting point for customization in accordance with local regulations.

To ensure that AI compliance policies are effectively adapted to each region, organizations should engage with local legal experts, regulators, and industry peers. These stakeholders can provide invaluable insights into the specific requirements of a given jurisdiction, as well as offer guidance on best practices for aligning AI policies with local norms and expectations. This collaborative approach not only helps ensure compliance but also fosters trust and credibility with local stakeholders.

Implementing a robust governance structure is another critical aspect of adapting AI compliance policies for global operations. This structure should facilitate centralized oversight and coordination of compliance efforts, while also allowing for flexibility in policy implementation at the regional level. This can be achieved by designating regional compliance officers or teams who are responsible for monitoring local regulatory developments, customizing AI policies to meet regional requirements, and liaising with the central compliance team to ensure that global standards are upheld.

Finally, organizations must remain vigilant in monitoring and reviewing their AI compliance policies to account for ongoing changes in the international regulatory landscape. Regular audits and assessments can help identify areas where policies may need updating or further customization, ensuring that businesses remain responsive to the evolving legal environment and maintain a strong commitment to responsible AI practices across their global operations.

CROSS-BORDER DATA PRIVACY AND SECURITY CONCERNS: MITIGATING RISKS AND UPHOLDING TRUST

In today's interconnected world, cross-border data transfers are an essential aspect of global business operations, particularly for organizations leveraging AI technologies. These transfers, however, pose significant challenges due to varying data privacy and security regulations across jurisdictions. Ensuring compliance with multiple sets of rules and mitigating risks associated with cross-border data flows are crucial to maintaining trust and credibility with stakeholders, including customers, partners, and regulatory authorities.

One of the key challenges in managing cross-border data privacy and security concerns is the complex web of laws and regulations governing data protection across different countries. The European Union's General Data Protection Regulation (GDPR) and the California Consumer Privacy Act (CCPA) in the United States are two prominent examples of stringent data privacy laws that have a significant impact on businesses operating across borders. Organizations must be aware of these and other relevant regulations and tailor their data handling practices to comply with the strictest standards applicable to their operations.

To effectively manage cross-border data privacy and security concerns, organizations should implement a comprehensive data protection framework that is adaptable to the unique requirements of each jurisdiction. This framework should encompass key elements such as data minimization, encryption, pseudonymization, and access controls to ensure that sensitive data is adequately protected throughout its lifecycle. Furthermore, organizations should conduct thorough risk assessments and establish clear protocols for responding to data breaches and other security incidents.

Another critical aspect of addressing cross-border data privacy and security concerns is fostering transparency and accountability in data handling practices. Organizations should clearly communicate their data protection policies to stakeholders and establish mechanisms for individuals to exercise their rights with respect to their personal data. Demonstrating a commitment to transparency and accountability can help build trust with customers and partners, mitigating reputational risks associated with cross-border data transfers.

Finally, organizations should consider leveraging data transfer mechanisms and agreements that have been recognized by regulatory authorities as providing adequate protection for personal data. Examples include the EU-US Privacy Shield (or its successor frameworks), Standard Contractual Clauses, and Binding Corporate Rules. By employing these mechanisms, organizations can ensure that they are meeting regulatory requirements for cross-border data transfers while also demonstrating their commitment to responsible data handling practices.

In summary, navigating cross-border data privacy and security concerns requires a proactive and adaptive approach that encompasses thorough understanding of relevant regulations, implementation of robust data protection measures, and a commitment to transparency and accountability. By addressing these concerns effectively, organizations can mitigate risks and uphold trust with stakeholders as they leverage AI technologies across borders.

FINAL THOUGHTS

The complex and ever-evolving landscape of global legal considerations poses a significant challenge for organizations implementing AI technologies. However, by proactively addressing these concerns, businesses can ensure compliance, mitigate risks, and build trust with stakeholders around the world. Navigating international AI regulations and guidelines, adapting AI compliance policies for global operations, and addressing cross-border data privacy and security concerns are all vital components of a robust global AI compliance strategy.

As AI continues to transform industries and reshape business operations, it is imperative for organizations to stay informed of the latest regulatory developments and best practices. By fostering a culture of continuous learning and adaptation, businesses can not only meet the compliance requirements of today but also anticipate and adapt to the emerging regulations of tomorrow.

Moreover, organizations should recognize the importance of collaborating with industry peers, regulatory bodies, and other stakeholders to share insights, discuss challenges, and contribute to the development of global AI compliance standards. This collaborative approach can help create a more resilient and responsible AI ecosystem that benefits all stakeholders.

In summary, embracing global compliance in AI is a key success factor for corporations operating in the international arena. By investing in robust AI compliance policies, training, monitoring, and continuous improvement efforts, businesses can unlock the full potential of AI technologies while maintaining trust, reducing risks, and promoting responsible innovation across borders.

CHAPTER 8

INDUSTRY-SPECIFIC AI COMPLIANCE: TAILORING STRATEGIES FOR UNIQUE CHALLENGES

As AI technology continues to make its way into various industries, it is crucial to recognize that each sector faces unique challenges and opportunities in the realm of AI compliance. From healthcare and finance to retail and manufacturing, different industries have distinct regulatory requirements and ethical considerations that must be addressed in a tailored manner.

In the healthcare sector, for example, AI applications have the potential to revolutionize diagnostics, treatment, and patient care. However, this industry is governed by strict regulations and guidelines aimed at protecting patient privacy and ensuring the safety and efficacy of medical treatments. AI compliance in healthcare must prioritize data privacy, patient confidentiality, and transparent decision-making processes to maintain trust and adhere to regulations like HIPAA and GDPR.

Similarly, the finance industry is using AI to improve fraud detection, risk management, and customer service. In this context, AI compliance requires a strong focus on data security, adherence to anti-money laundering (AML) and know-your-customer (KYC) regulations, as well as transparency in algorithmic decision-making to prevent discrimination and bias in financial services.

In retail and manufacturing, AI is transforming supply chain management, inventory control, and personalized marketing efforts. Compliance in these industries must address concerns surrounding data privacy, labor rights, and environmental impacts, while also adhering to industry-specific regulations and guidelines.

When developing an AI compliance strategy, organizations must carefully consider the unique challenges and requirements of their specific industry. By engaging with industry-specific regulations, guidelines, and best practices, businesses can design and implement AI compliance policies that are not only effective and robust but also tailored to the particular needs and concerns of their sector. This customized approach to AI compliance will ultimately enable organizations to harness the full potential of AI technologies while minimizing risks and maximizing stakeholder trust.

Addressing Unique Compliance Requirements in Various Industries: A Holistic Approach

Successfully addressing unique compliance requirements in various industries necessitates a holistic approach that combines an understanding of sector-specific regulations, ethical considerations, and best practices. Organizations must develop strategies to adapt and evolve their AI compliance policies as the landscape changes, ensuring they remain up-to-date and effective in meeting the specific needs of their industry.

First, organizations must become intimately familiar with the regulatory landscape governing their industry. This includes not only understanding the current legal requirements but also staying informed on emerging regulations and guidelines that may impact AI implementation. By engaging with industry associations, regulatory bodies, and legal experts, organizations can ensure they maintain a strong foundation in the evolving regulatory environment.

Next, organizations must prioritize ethical considerations unique to their industry. For example, AI applications in healthcare must consider patient privacy and data protection, while those in finance must address issues of fairness and bias in decision-making. By embedding ethical principles into the design, development, and deployment of AI systems, organizations can mitigate potential risks and foster trust among stakeholders.

Collaboration with other industry players and regulatory bodies is essential in addressing unique compliance requirements. By participating in industry forums and working groups, organizations can share best practices, discuss common challenges, and collectively develop industry-wide standards for AI compliance. This collaborative approach allows companies to learn from each other's experiences and adapt to new compliance challenges more effectively.

Organizations should also invest in AI compliance training that is tailored to their industry. By providing employees with targeted education on the specific risks, regulations, and ethical considerations in their field, organizations can build a culture of compliance that permeates every level of the company.

Finally, organizations must continuously evaluate and refine their AI compliance policies and processes to ensure they remain effective and aligned with industry requirements. Regular audits, feedback from employees and stakeholders, and monitoring of industry trends will enable organizations to identify areas for improvement and adapt their strategies accordingly.

Addressing unique compliance requirements in various industries requires a holistic approach that encompasses regulatory understanding, ethical considerations, collaboration, tailored training, and continuous improvement. By adopting this comprehensive strategy, organizations can effectively navigate the complex world of AI compliance while reaping the benefits of AI technology within their industry.

Adapting AI Policies and Training to Industry-Specific Contexts: A Practical Approach

In an era where AI technology is increasingly prevalent across various industries, organizations must adapt their AI policies and training programs to address the unique challenges and requirements of their specific contexts. A practical approach to this process ensures that organizations maintain compliance with industry regulations while promoting ethical AI use and maximizing its potential benefits.

To begin adapting AI policies and training to industry-specific contexts, organizations should conduct a thorough assessment of their current AI applications and identify any regulatory, ethical, or operational challenges that may arise within their industry. This assessment should consider factors such as data privacy, bias and fairness, transparency, and accountability, as well as any unique regulations that apply to the organization's operations.

Once the organization has a clear understanding of its industry-specific challenges, it can begin to tailor its AI policies and procedures accordingly. This may involve developing new guidelines, updating existing policies, or implementing additional oversight mechanisms to ensure compliance with relevant regulations and ethical principles. Organizations should also engage with industry experts, peers, and regulators to stay informed of best practices and emerging trends.

Training programs must also be adapted to address the unique needs of each industry. By incorporating industry-specific case studies, real-world examples, and scenarios into training materials, organizations can provide employees with a more targeted understanding of AI compliance issues and best practices in their field. This targeted training approach helps employees better grasp the nuances of AI applications in their industry and fosters a culture of compliance throughout the organization.

In addition to tailoring training content, organizations should also consider the most effective training methodologies for their industry. For instance, industries with rapidly changing regulations may benefit from frequent, modular training sessions, while those with more stable environments might opt for in-depth, annual training programs. By selecting the most appropriate training methodology, organizations can ensure employees receive timely and relevant education.

Finally, organizations should establish a feedback loop to continuously improve and adapt their AI policies and training programs as industry contexts evolve. By soliciting feedback from employees, stakeholders, and regulators, as well as monitoring industry trends, organizations can identify areas for improvement and make the necessary adjustments to remain compliant and effective.

Adapting AI policies and training to industry-specific contexts is a crucial aspect of AI compliance. Through a practical approach that includes assessment, tailored policies, targeted training, and continuous improvement, organizations can ensure they effectively address the unique challenges of their industry and harness the full potential of AI technology.

BEST PRACTICES FOR MANAGING INDUSTRY-SPECIFIC AI RISKS: A COMPREHENSIVE GUIDE

As organizations increasingly adopt AI technology across various industries, managing industry-specific AI risks becomes a critical aspect of maintaining compliance and ensuring ethical AI use. By adopting best practices, organizations can mitigate potential risks, maximize the benefits of AI, and create a culture of compliance and responsibility. This section outlines several best practices for managing industry-specific AI risks.

1. Conduct regular risk assessments: Regularly evaluate your organization's AI systems and applications to identify potential risks and vulnerabilities. Assess the AI landscape within your industry to stay informed about emerging trends, chal-

lenges, and regulatory changes. By proactively identifying risks, organizations can take necessary steps to mitigate them before they become critical issues.

2. Develop clear AI policies and guidelines: Establish comprehensive AI policies and guidelines that address industry-specific risks and regulatory requirements. These policies should encompass data privacy, bias and fairness, transparency, accountability, and any other ethical considerations relevant to your industry. Regularly review and update these policies to keep them current and effective.

3. Implement strong governance and oversight: Establish a robust governance structure, including a dedicated AI ethics committee or an AI compliance officer, to oversee AI-related initiatives and ensure compliance with industry regulations and ethical standards. This structure should also facilitate collaboration between various departments and stakeholders to ensure a holistic approach to managing AI risks.

4. Foster a culture of compliance and responsibility: Encourage a culture of compliance and responsibility throughout the organization by providing ongoing training and education on AI ethics and compliance. Empower employees to raise concerns, ask questions, and contribute to the development of ethical AI practices within your organization.

5. Collaborate with industry peers and regulatory bodies: Engage with other organizations, industry associations, and regulatory bodies to share knowledge, discuss best practices,

and stay informed about evolving industry standards and regulations. This collaborative approach can help organizations navigate complex AI compliance landscapes and mitigate risks more effectively.

6. Adopt a proactive approach to AI risk management: Rather than reacting to risks as they emerge, adopt a proactive approach by anticipating potential issues and taking preventive measures. This may involve conducting regular AI audits, implementing AI monitoring tools, and setting up early warning systems to detect potential problems.

7. Ensure transparency and explainability: Develop transparent AI systems that can be easily understood and audited by stakeholders, including regulators and customers. Invest in explainable AI technologies that can provide insights into how AI systems make decisions, helping organizations address potential biases and ethical concerns.

8. Continuously monitor AI systems: Implement continuous monitoring of AI systems to identify potential risks, biases, and other issues in real-time. Use AI-powered analytics tools to gain insights into system performance and detect anomalies that may indicate potential problems.

9. Conduct third-party audits: Engage external experts to perform independent audits of your AI systems, policies, and practices. Third-party audits can provide valuable insights and unbiased assessments of your organization's AI risk management strategies.

Effectively managing industry-specific AI risks requires a comprehensive and proactive approach. By adopting best practices, organizations can minimize potential risks, ensure compliance with industry regulations, and maintain ethical AI practices, ultimately driving AI innovation and growth within their industry.

FINAL THOUGHTS

Understanding and addressing industry-specific AI compliance is essential for organizations seeking to harness the power of AI technology while minimizing risks and ensuring ethical practices. By identifying unique compliance requirements, tailoring AI policies and training programs to the specific context of their industry, and implementing best practices for managing AI risks, organizations can create a strong foundation for ethical and responsible AI use.

Moreover, fostering a culture of compliance and responsibility, collaborating with industry peers and regulatory bodies, and staying up-to-date on legal and corporate concerns related to AI will enable organizations to remain agile and adaptable in the face of evolving regulations and technology advancements. Continuous improvement and adaptation arc kcy factors in successfully navigating the complex landscape of AI compliance and reaping the benefits of AI innovation.

As the AI landscape continues to evolve, it is essential for organizations to be proactive in their approach to AI compliance and risk management. By remaining vigilant, engaging in ongoing training and education, and committing to industry-specific compliance, organizations can unlock the full potential of AI technology and drive growth, efficiency, and success in their respective industries.

CHAPTER 9

AI COMPLIANCE IN THE PUBLIC SECTOR: BUILDING TRUST AND ENSURING TRANSPARENCY

As AI TECHNOLOGY CONTINUES TO RESHAPE THE PUBLIC sector, it is essential to acknowledge the unique challenges and responsibilities faced by government agencies and organizations in implementing AI solutions. This chapter will explore the importance of AI compliance in the public sector, focusing on the need to build trust, ensure transparency, and promote ethical AI practices in the delivery of public services.

The public sector is tasked with the critical responsibility of serving citizens and protecting their interests. As such, AI compliance in this context goes beyond adhering to legal and regulatory requirements; it must also encompass ethical considerations, data privacy, and security concerns, as well as issues related to fairness, accountability, and transparency. By establishing and maintaining robust AI compliance programs, public sector organizations can foster a positive and responsible relationship with AI, enabling them to harness its potential for improving the delivery of services and enhancing the lives of citizens.

Ensuring AI Compliance within Government Agencies: A Path to Responsible AI Adoption

Government agencies face unique challenges when it comes to implementing AI solutions, as they must strike a balance between innovation and the protection of citizens' rights. Ensuring AI compliance within government agencies is essential to responsibly harness the power of AI while maintaining the public trust. This section will delve into the key components of establishing and maintaining an AI compliance framework within government agencies, fostering a culture of responsibility and transparency.

Firstly, government agencies must develop clear policies and guidelines that outline ethical principles and set expectations for AI use within their organizations. These guidelines should address concerns such as data privacy, algorithmic transparency, and bias mitigation, ensuring that AI systems are developed and deployed in a manner that respects citizens' rights and serves the public interest.

Next, government agencies should invest in AI training programs for their employees, enabling them to better understand the implications of AI technology and make informed decisions about its deployment. These training programs should include both technical and non-technical aspects, ensuring that employees across the organization are equipped to contribute to AI compliance efforts.

Collaboration with external stakeholders, such as industry partners, academia, and civil society organizations, is also crucial for government agencies to stay abreast of the latest developments in AI technology and compliance. By fostering an open dialogue with these stakeholders, government agencies can benefit from diverse perspectives and insights, enabling them to develop more robust and effective AI compliance frameworks.

Finally, continuous monitoring and evaluation of AI systems are essential to ensure ongoing compliance with established guidelines and policies. Government agencies should implement processes for regular audits and assessments of their AI solutions, allowing them to identify and address any potential compliance issues proactively.

By adhering to these principles, government agencies can promote responsible AI adoption within their organizations, ensuring that they harness the benefits of AI technology while safeguarding the rights and interests of the citizens they serve.

Balancing Innovation with Accountability and Transparency: The Key to Responsible AI Adoption

As AI continues to transform industries and redefine the way we live and work, striking a balance between innovation, accountability, and transparency has become increasingly vital. In this section, we will explore the importance of this balance in the context of AI adoption and outline the best practices for organizations to ensure they maximize the potential of AI while adhering to ethical principles and maintaining public trust.

Innovation is at the core of AI's promise to revolutionize various aspects of our lives, from healthcare to transportation. As organizations embrace AI to gain a competitive edge and drive growth, they must be cautious not to overlook the potential risks associated with the technology. Balancing innovation with accountability and transparency is essential to ensure that AI systems are developed and deployed ethically, minimizing adverse consequences and fostering trust.

To achieve this balance, organizations should prioritize the following best practices:

1. Develop clear AI governance policies: Establishing a strong governance framework is essential to guide AI development and deployment processes. This framework should include clear policies outlining the organization's commit-

ment to ethical AI, as well as specific guidelines on topics such as data privacy, algorithmic fairness, and explainability.

2. Foster a culture of ethical AI: Encouraging a culture of responsible AI adoption starts at the top, with leadership demonstrating a commitment to ethical principles. This culture should extend throughout the organization, ensuring that employees at all levels are aware of and adhere to AI ethics guidelines.

3. Invest in AI training and education: Equipping employees with the necessary knowledge and skills to understand AI technology and its implications is crucial for responsible AI adoption. Organizations should invest in comprehensive training programs that cover both technical and ethical aspects of AI.

4. Engage with external stakeholders: Collaboration with external stakeholders, such as regulatory bodies, industry peers, and academic institutions, can provide valuable insights and guidance on AI compliance best practices. Organizations should actively participate in industry forums and seek external expert opinions to enhance their AI compliance efforts.

5. Implement monitoring and auditing mechanisms: Continuous monitoring of AI systems is vital to ensure ongoing compliance with ethical guidelines and to identify potential risks or issues. Organizations should establish regular auditing and reporting processes to assess their AI solutions' performance and compliance with established policies.

By adhering to these best practices, organizations can balance the drive for innovation with the need for accountability and transparency, ensuring that AI technology serves as a force for good and builds public trust.

Addressing Public Sector-Specific AI Challenges and Opportunities: Maximizing Benefits while Minimizing Risks

In the public sector, AI holds enormous potential to transform service delivery, streamline processes, and address pressing societal challenges. However, with great potential come unique challenges and opportunities that public sector organizations must navigate to maximize the benefits while minimizing risks. In this section, we will explore these challenges and opportunities, and provide practical recommendations for public sector entities to ensure responsible AI adoption.

Some of the primary challenges that the public sector faces in the context of AI compliance include:

1. Data privacy and security: Public sector organizations handle sensitive data, making it crucial to safeguard citizens' privacy and comply with data protection regulations. AI systems must be designed to ensure the secure handling and storage of data, as well as provide transparency on how this information is used.

2. Algorithmic fairness and bias: The public sector's deci-

sions can have far-reaching consequences for citizens. AI systems must be free of biases and ensure that algorithmic decision-making is fair, equitable, and non-discriminatory.

3. Explainability and transparency: As public sector organizations deploy AI systems, it is essential to maintain transparency in decision-making processes. AI systems should be explainable, enabling organizations to provide clear justifications for their decisions.

4. Accountability and oversight: Public sector organizations must establish clear lines of accountability and oversight to ensure that AI systems adhere to ethical guidelines and legal requirements.

To address these challenges and seize the opportunities presented by AI, public sector organizations should consider the following recommendations:

1. Establish cross-functional AI teams: Assembling a diverse team of experts, including data scientists, legal advisors, and ethics specialists, will help ensure a holistic approach to AI adoption, taking into account technical, legal, and ethical considerations.

2. Collaborate with other public sector organizations: Sharing knowledge, resources, and best practices among public sector entities can lead to more effective and efficient AI adoption. Cooperation at the local, regional, and international levels can help address common challenges and create synergies.

3. Engage with the private sector and academia: Forming partnerships with private sector organizations and academic institutions can bring valuable expertise, resources, and innovative solutions to the public sector's AI adoption efforts.

4. Focus on citizen-centric AI applications: Public sector organizations should prioritize AI applications that directly benefit citizens, such as improving service delivery, enhancing public safety, and addressing critical societal challenges like climate change and healthcare.

5. Invest in AI education and awareness: Raising awareness and understanding of AI technology among public sector employees and the general public is essential for responsible AI adoption. Investing in training programs and educational initiatives can help create a more informed and engaged citizenry.

By addressing these challenges and capitalizing on the opportunities, public sector organizations can harness the power of AI to deliver better services, drive innovation, and ultimately improve the quality of life for citizens.

FINAL THOUGHTS

As we conclude this chapter, it is essential to reiterate the immense potential that AI holds for the public sector. From improved service delivery and resource optimization to addressing pressing societal challenges, AI can be a powerful catalyst for positive change. However, realizing this potential requires responsible AI adoption that adheres to the highest standards of compliance, fairness, transparency, and accountability.

Throughout this chapter, we have explored various aspects of AI compliance in the public sector, ranging from data privacy and security to ensuring algorithmic fairness and addressing sector-specific challenges. We have also shared recommendations and best practices that public sector organizations can adopt as they navigate the complex landscape of AI adoption.

In summary, it is crucial for public sector organizations to strike the right balance between harnessing AI's benefits and mitigating its risks. To achieve this balance, organizations must develop and implement robust AI compliance policies that take into account legal, ethical, and technical considerations. They must also invest in comprehensive AI training programs for employees, fostering a culture of compliance and continuous learning. Establishing strong partnerships with private sector organizations, academia, and other public sector entities is equally important, as it promotes collaboration and knowledge-sharing. Finally, organizations need to continuously monitor and adapt AI policies and practices to stay current with evolving regulations, industry trends, and technological advancements. By embracing AI compliance, public sector organizations can ensure the responsible and effective use of AI to create a better future for all.

CHAPTER 10

NAVIGATING THE DYNAMIC LANDSCAPE OF AI COMPLIANCE IN THE FUTURE

As we continue to witness rapid advancements in AI and machine learning, their applications in various industries and the public sector are expanding exponentially. This presents new challenges and opportunities in the realm of AI compliance. In this chapter, we delve into the future of AI compliance, discussing the emerging trends, technological innovations, and regulatory shifts that will shape the AI landscape in the coming years. Our goal is to provide a comprehensive understanding of what lies ahead, equipping corporations with the knowledge and insights necessary to navigate the evolving world of AI compliance effectively and responsibly.

EMERGING TRENDS AND TECHNOLOGIES SHAPING AI COMPLIANCE

The future of AI compliance is undoubtedly intertwined with the developments in AI technologies and the evolving trends in the field. Among these trends is the growing need for explainable AI, which focuses on making AI systems more transparent and understandable for humans. As AI systems become increasingly complex, explainable AI will play a crucial role in ensuring that organizations maintain trust, meet regulatory requirements, and avoid biases and errors.

Another significant trend is the increased use of AI-powered tools to monitor and enforce compliance. Such tools enable real-time compliance checks, risk assessments, and remediation actions, allowing organizations to stay ahead of potential violations and legal issues. Moreover, the growing importance of privacy-preserving AI technologies, such as federated learning and differential privacy, will help organizations address the challenges related to cross-border data privacy and security.

In addition to these trends, we can expect the emergence of new regulatory frameworks and guidelines, both on national and international levels. As a result, organizations must be prepared to adapt their AI compliance policies and practices to accommodate these changing regulations. By staying informed and leveraging cutting-edge AI compliance technologies, corporations can not only ensure compliance but also gain a competitive advantage in the marketplace.

Preparing for the Evolving Regulatory Landscape

As the AI industry continues to expand and mature, businesses can expect the regulatory landscape to evolve alongside it. To ensure compliance and maintain a strong competitive edge, organizations must be proactive in their approach to understanding and adapting to these changes. One way to prepare for the evolving regulatory landscape is to establish a dedicated team or designate a compliance officer responsible for staying informed on legal developments and emerging guidelines. This team should engage in regular discussions with legal experts, industry peers, and regulators to remain up-to-date on the latest trends.

Additionally, organizations should implement agile and flexible AI compliance policies that can be easily updated to reflect new requirements. This flexibility is essential for maintaining compliance, as it allows for the swift incorporation of changes without disrupting ongoing operations. Companies should also invest in employee training and awareness programs that emphasize the importance of compliance and educate team members on the latest regulations.

Finally, organizations should actively participate in industry events and forums, contributing to the dialogue surrounding AI compliance and regulation. By engaging with policymakers, regulators, and other stakeholders, companies can help shape the regulatory landscape to better suit their needs and encourage industry-wide best practices. Through proactive preparation, businesses can successfully navigate the evolving regulatory landscape and maintain a robust AI compliance strategy.

DEVELOPING A PROACTIVE APPROACH TO FUTURE AI COMPLIANCE CHALLENGES

To effectively address future AI compliance challenges, organizations must adopt a proactive approach that involves anticipating potential issues and implementing preventive measures. Developing a forward-thinking strategy requires a deep understanding of the AI landscape and an awareness of emerging trends, regulations, and technologies.

First and foremost, businesses should establish a culture of continuous learning and improvement, encouraging employees to stay informed on AI advancements and compliance requirements. This includes conducting regular training sessions, sharing industry news and insights, and fostering open communication about compliance-related concerns. By nurturing a proactive mindset, organizations can better anticipate potential compliance issues and swiftly address them.

Second, organizations should actively participate in industry forums, conferences, and workshops to stay ahead of the curve on AI developments and regulations. Building relationships with regulators, industry peers, and legal experts can provide valuable insights into the future of AI compliance and help organizations prepare for upcoming changes.

Third, businesses should prioritize investment in AI-powered monitoring and analysis tools that can detect compliance gaps and potential violations in real-time. These tools can not only help organizations quickly identify and address issues, but also provide valuable data to inform ongoing policy and training refinements.

Lastly, organizations should regularly review and update their AI compliance policies to ensure they remain aligned with current industry standards and regulations. This process should involve soliciting feedback from employees, stakeholders, and experts, and incorporating their insights to make the necessary adjustments.

By adopting a proactive approach to future AI compliance challenges, businesses can not only safeguard themselves against potential violations but also position themselves as leaders in the rapidly evolving world of AI.

FINAL THOUGHTS

As we conclude this exploration of the future of AI compliance, it is clear that staying ahead of the curve in this rapidly evolving landscape is essential for organizations seeking long-term success. By embracing emerging trends and technologies, preparing for the evolving regulatory landscape, and developing a proactive approach to future AI compliance challenges, businesses can effectively navigate the complexities of AI compliance while fostering innovation and growth.

Throughout this book, we have discussed various aspects of AI compliance, including policy development, employee training, monitoring and check-ins, industry-specific compliance, and global legal considerations. Each of these components plays a critical role in creating a comprehensive and effective AI compliance strategy, which is crucial for organizations as they strive to maintain ethical and responsible AI practices.

In closing, it is important to recognize that AI compliance is not a one-time effort but rather an ongoing process that requires continuous improvement and adaptation. As new technologies emerge and regulations change, organizations must remain agile and committed to fostering a culture of compliance, learning, and collaboration. By doing so, they can not only ensure their own success but also contribute to the responsible growth and development of the AI ecosystem.

CHAPTER 11

MEASURING THE IMPACT OF AI COMPLIANCE EXCELLENCE

As ORGANIZATIONS INCREASINGLY ADOPT ARTIFICIAL intelligence technologies, the importance of implementing robust AI compliance programs cannot be overstated. However, merely establishing a compliance program is not enough—organizations must also be able to measure the impact of their AI compliance excellence to understand its effectiveness and continuously improve their practices. This chapter will explore various aspects of assessing the impact of AI compliance, from evaluating the effectiveness of training programs to identifying key performance indicators (KPIs) that align with organizational objectives. By understanding the outcomes of their AI compliance efforts, organizations can make informed decisions, refine their strategies, and ultimately achieve a higher level of AI compliance excellence.

EVALUATING COMPLIANCE PERFORMANCE METRICS

The foundation of a successful AI compliance program is the ability to accurately evaluate its performance. By tracking and analyzing relevant compliance performance metrics, organizations can gain valuable insights into the effectiveness of their policies, training programs, and overall compliance strategy. Key performance indicators (KPIs) should be carefully chosen to align with organizational objectives and regulatory requirements, ensuring that the metrics accurately reflect the organization's progress toward achieving AI compliance excellence.

Examples of AI compliance performance metrics include the number of AI-related incidents, the frequency of compliance audits, and the percentage of employees who have completed AI compliance training. Additionally, organizations may track the speed of incident resolution and the number of regulatory inquiries or penalties incurred. By regularly reviewing these metrics, organizations can identify trends, uncover areas for improvement, and adjust their compliance strategies accordingly. Furthermore, comparing industry benchmarks and best practices can provide valuable context and help organizations set ambitious, yet realistic, goals for their AI compliance initiatives.

Assessing the Return on Investment in AI Compliance Initiatives

An essential aspect of evaluating AI compliance initiatives is determining their return on investment (ROI). By understanding the ROI of AI compliance efforts, organizations can ensure that they are allocating resources effectively and achieving the desired outcomes. Assessing the ROI involves quantifying the benefits derived from AI compliance initiatives, such as reduced regulatory penalties, increased operational efficiency, and enhanced brand reputation, and comparing these benefits to the costs of implementing and maintaining the compliance program.

One approach to calculating the ROI of AI compliance initiatives is to consider both direct and indirect benefits. Direct benefits may include the avoidance of fines and sanctions, decreased legal fees, and reduced costs associated with compliance violations. Indirect benefits, on the other hand, can be more challenging to quantify but may encompass improved stakeholder trust, greater employee engagement, and a more proactive approach to risk management.

To accurately assess the ROI of AI compliance initiatives, organizations should establish a baseline of their compliance performance before implementing new policies or programs. This baseline can then be compared to the post-implementation performance to measure the impact of the initiatives. By tracking the ROI of AI compliance efforts over time, organizations can demonstrate the value of their investments, justify the allocation of resources, and make informed decisions about future compliance strategies.

IDENTIFYING AREAS FOR FUTURE GROWTH AND DEVELOPMENT

As the AI landscape continues to evolve, it is crucial for organizations to identify areas for future growth and development in their compliance initiatives. By proactively addressing potential challenges and capitalizing on emerging opportunities, organizations can remain at the forefront of AI compliance excellence. To do this, it is important to keep an eye on the latest technological advancements, regulatory changes, and industry trends that could impact AI compliance efforts.

One approach to identifying areas for future growth and development is through regular environmental scanning, which involves monitoring and analyzing external factors that could influence the organization's AI compliance program. This process can help organizations anticipate changes in the regulatory landscape, understand emerging risks and opportunities, and adapt their compliance strategies accordingly.

Another key aspect of identifying areas for future growth and development is leveraging feedback from internal and external stakeholders, including employees, customers, regulators, and industry peers. By engaging in open dialogue and fostering a culture of continuous improvement, organizations can gain valuable insights into areas where their AI compliance initiatives can be enhanced or expanded.

Lastly, organizations should consider benchmarking their AI compliance efforts against industry best practices and standards. By comparing their performance to that of their peers, organizations can identify gaps, areas of strength, and potential opportunities for growth and development. This process can also help organizations prioritize their compliance investments and allocate resources strategically to maximize their impact.

Identifying areas for future growth and development in AI compliance is an ongoing process that requires organizations to remain agile and adaptive. By staying informed, engaging stakeholders, and benchmarking against industry best practices, organizations can ensure their AI compliance programs continue to drive value and foster a culture of excellence.

BENCHMARKING AI COMPLIANCE PERFORMANCE AGAINST INDUSTRY STANDARDS

Benchmarking is a critical process in AI compliance management, as it allows organizations to measure their compliance performance against industry standards and best practices. By comparing their AI policies, practices, and performance to that of their peers, organizations can identify areas of strength and opportunities for improvement, ensuring they remain competitive and compliant in an ever-evolving regulatory landscape.

To effectively benchmark AI compliance performance, organizations should start by identifying relevant industry standards, guidelines, and best practices. These may include international frameworks, such as the OECD AI Principles, sector-specific guidelines, or recommendations from industry associations and expert groups. In addition to formal standards, organizations should also consider informal best practices shared by industry peers and thought leaders.

Once relevant benchmarks have been identified, organizations should evaluate their current AI compliance policies and practices against these standards. This may involve assessing the comprehensiveness of their AI compliance program, the effectiveness of their training initiatives, the adequacy of their monitoring and reporting systems, and the extent to which they are addressing industry-specific risks and challenges.

Upon completing the benchmarking process, organizations should analyze the results to identify gaps, areas of strength, and potential opportunities for improvement. It is important to recognize that benchmarking is not a one-time exercise but rather an ongoing process that should be periodically revisited to ensure continued alignment with industry standards and evolving best practices.

Benchmarking AI compliance performance against industry standards is a valuable tool for organizations seeking to maintain a robust and effective compliance program. By regularly comparing their AI policies and practices to those of their peers, organizations can gain insights into areas where their compliance efforts can be enhanced, ensuring they remain at the forefront of AI compliance excellence.

Final Thoughts

In this chapter, we have explored various aspects of measuring the impact of AI compliance excellence. From evaluating compliance performance metrics and assessing the return on investment in AI compliance initiatives to identifying areas for future growth and development, we have emphasized the importance of a proactive and data-driven approach to AI compliance management.

Benchmarking against industry standards is a crucial part of this process, as it allows organizations to gauge their performance relative to peers and best practices, helping them stay competitive and compliant in a rapidly evolving regulatory environment. By continually monitoring, analyzing, and adapting their AI compliance policies, practices, and performance, organizations can ensure that they are well-prepared for the challenges and opportunities that lie ahead.

As AI continues to play an increasingly important role in

our lives and businesses, the need for robust and effective AI compliance programs will only grow more pressing. By adopting the strategies and best practices outlined in this chapter, organizations can not only mitigate the risks associated with AI but also capitalize on the immense potential that this transformative technology has to offer.

Conclusion

As we reach the conclusion of this book, it is clear that AI training and compliance are integral components of the modern corporate landscape. The rapid growth and widespread adoption of AI technologies have significantly impacted businesses across all industries, presenting both unparalleled opportunities and unprecedented challenges. By understanding the intricacies of AI compliance and diligently implementing effective strategies, organizations can mitigate risks, adhere to legal and ethical standards, and ensure responsible AI deployment.

Throughout this book, we have delved into various aspects of AI compliance, including policy development, employee training, ongoing monitoring, industry-specific considerations, and future trends. We have emphasized the importance of fostering a culture of compliance, continuous learning, and proactive adaptation to the evolving AI landscape.

Ultimately, success in AI compliance depends on a holistic approach that encompasses regulatory, technical, and organizational aspects. Collaboration among stakeholders, industry peers, and regulatory bodies is key to developing best practices and staying informed of the latest developments. By embracing change, investing in continuous improvement, and leveraging intelligence reports, organizations can stay ahead in the rapidly changing AI landscape and harness the full potential of AI while maintaining the highest standards of ethical and legal compliance.

As AI continues to transform our world, it is our responsibility as organizations, professionals, and individuals to ensure that we harness its power responsibly, ethically, and in the best interests of all stakeholders. With the insights and guidance provided in this book, we hope to have equipped you with the knowledge and tools necessary to navigate the complex terrain of AI compliance with confidence and success.

THE VITAL ROLE OF AI COMPLIANCE EXCELLENCE IN DRIVING BUSINESS SUCCESS

The emergence of AI technologies has revolutionized the way businesses operate, providing unprecedented opportunities to improve efficiency, enhance decision-making, and

create new revenue streams. However, alongside these transformative benefits come complex legal, ethical, and regulatory challenges. The pursuit of AI Compliance Excellence is
not only crucial for mitigating risks, but also serves as a key
driver for long-term business success.

AI Compliance Excellence ensures that organizations
maintain a strong reputation by demonstrating a commitment to ethical AI practices. In today's increasingly interconnected and transparent world, ethical lapses can have
far-reaching consequences, damaging a company's brand
image, customer trust, and financial performance. By
adhering to stringent AI compliance standards, businesses
can uphold their reputation and maintain a competitive
edge in the market.

Moreover, a robust AI compliance framework fosters
innovation by providing clear guidelines for the responsible
development and deployment of AI technologies. By
addressing potential risks and pitfalls at the outset, organizations can mitigate the chance of costly setbacks and ensure
that their AI initiatives align with legal and ethical standards. This proactive approach to AI compliance enables
businesses to unlock the full potential of AI technologies
while minimizing risk.

Furthermore, AI Compliance Excellence contributes to
long-term financial sustainability by reducing the likelihood
of fines, lawsuits, and regulatory penalties arising from non-
compliance. The costs associated with non-compliant AI
practices can be significant, including financial losses,

wasted resources, and damaged relationships with regulators, customers, and other stakeholders. By investing in AI
compliance, organizations can protect their bottom line and
focus on driving business growth.

AI Compliance Excellence plays a vital role in driving
business success by safeguarding reputation, fostering innovation, and ensuring financial sustainability. By incorporating robust AI compliance frameworks and practices,
organizations can navigate the complex AI landscape with
confidence and fully harness the transformative power of AI
technologies to fuel their long-term growth and success.

THE ONGOING JOURNEY TOWARD AI COMPLIANCE MASTERY

The pursuit of AI Compliance Mastery is a continuous and
evolving journey, as businesses navigate the rapidly changing
landscape of AI technologies, regulations, and ethical
considerations. Achieving mastery in AI compliance
requires organizations to adopt a proactive mindset,
embrace a culture of continuous learning, and stay
informed about the latest developments in AI and
compliance.

Central to this ongoing journey is the cultivation of a
culture of compliance, which encourages employees at all
levels to prioritize ethical and responsible AI practices. This
involves fostering open communication channels, providing
ongoing training, and supporting a culture of shared

responsibility. By promoting a strong compliance culture, organizations can ensure that AI-related decisions are made with a thorough understanding of legal and ethical implications, reducing the likelihood of breaches and non-compliant behavior.

Another crucial aspect of the journey toward AI Compliance Mastery is the continuous monitoring and improvement of AI systems, policies, and practices. As AI technologies evolve and new regulatory frameworks emerge, organizations must be agile in their response, updating their compliance programs and training to reflect the latest developments. By engaging in regular audits, risk assessments, and performance evaluations, businesses can identify potential areas of weakness, address them proactively, and drive continuous improvement.

Collaboration also plays a key role in the ongoing pursuit of AI Compliance Mastery. By working closely with industry peers, regulatory bodies, and other stakeholders, organizations can share best practices, learn from one another's experiences, and stay up-to-date with emerging trends and challenges. Additionally, engaging in open dialogue with stakeholders and employees can provide valuable insights that inform future policy and training improvements.

Finally, embracing the spirit of innovation is essential in the journey toward AI Compliance Mastery. As organizations continue to explore the potential of AI technologies, they must balance the drive for innovation with a commitment to ethical and responsible practices. By striking this balance, businesses can ensure that their AI initiatives create value while adhering to the highest standards of compliance.

The ongoing journey toward AI Compliance Mastery is characterized by a commitment to continuous learning, improvement, and collaboration. By cultivating a strong compliance culture, staying informed, and embracing innovation, organizations can successfully navigate the complex world of AI compliance and harness the transformative power of AI technologies to drive long-term success.

FUTURE OUTLOOK AND POTENTIAL DEVELOPMENTS IN AI COMPLIANCE

As AI technologies continue to evolve and permeate various aspects of business operations, the field of AI compliance is set to experience significant developments and transformations. This section explores the potential future outlook and emerging trends in AI compliance that organizations should monitor and prepare for.

One key development in AI compliance is the increasing complexity and sophistication of AI models, including the rise of deep learning, reinforcement learning, and other advanced techniques. These complex models may pose new challenges for compliance, as their decision-making processes can be more opaque and difficult to explain. As a result, organizations will need to adopt new strategies for ensuring transparency, accountability, and explainability in their AI systems, such as deploying advanced interpretability methods or adopting new approaches to model auditing and validation.

Another potential development is the emergence of new regulatory frameworks and industry standards, both at the national and international levels. As governments and regulatory bodies continue to grapple with the ethical, legal, and societal implications of AI technologies, we can expect an increase in regulations and guidelines governing AI use. Organizations must remain vigilant and adaptive, updating their compliance programs and policies to stay in step with these evolving frameworks.

Additionally, the future of AI compliance will likely involve greater collaboration between organizations, regulatory bodies, and other stakeholders. This collaboration may take the form of industry-specific consortia, cross-border regulatory initiatives, or public-private partnerships, all aimed at developing best practices, sharing knowledge, and promoting responsible AI adoption. By engaging in these collaborative efforts, organizations can stay ahead of the curve and ensure they are well-equipped to tackle emerging AI compliance challenges.

The role of AI-powered tools and technologies in compliance management is also expected to grow. Advanced analytics, machine learning, and natural language processing capabilities can help organizations monitor compliance more effectively, detect potential violations, and streamline reporting and remediation processes. As these tools become more sophisticated and widely adopted, organizations will need to invest in their integration and deployment to maintain a competitive edge in AI compliance.

Finally, the future of AI compliance will likely involve a more proactive, risk-based approach to compliance management. Instead of merely reacting to compliance breaches and violations, organizations will need to develop strategies for identifying and mitigating risks before they materialize. This may involve greater emphasis on risk assessments, stress testing, and scenario analysis, as well as the development of more robust internal controls and monitoring systems.

The future of AI compliance promises to be marked by significant advancements and changes, from the increasing complexity of AI models to the emergence of new regulatory frameworks and industry standards. Organizations must remain agile, adaptive, and proactive in their approach to AI compliance, embracing collaboration, innovation, and continuous improvement to thrive in this rapidly evolving landscape.

Encouraging a Proactive and Collaborative Approach to AI Compliance in the Industry

A proactive and collaborative approach to AI compliance is crucial for organizations to navigate the ever-evolving landscape of AI technologies and regulations. This section highlights the importance of fostering a proactive mindset and establishing effective collaborations within the industry to drive AI compliance excellence.

Organizations should prioritize a proactive approach to AI compliance by emphasizing ongoing risk assessments, continuous improvement, and staying abreast of emerging trends and technologies. By adopting this mindset, companies can identify potential compliance challenges before they materialize, allowing them to develop mitigation strategies and ensure that their AI systems remain aligned with ethical, legal, and societal norms. A proactive approach also enables organizations to identify opportunities for leveraging AI technologies to streamline and enhance their compliance management processes, ultimately driving efficiency and competitive advantage.

Collaboration plays a key role in the success of AI compliance efforts, as it fosters knowledge sharing, innovation, and the development of best practices. Organizations should actively engage with industry peers, regulatory bodies, and other stakeholders to stay informed about new developments in AI regulations, guidelines, and industry standards. This can be achieved through participation in industry forums, conferences, and working groups, or by forming strategic partnerships with relevant organizations.

Cross-sector collaboration is also essential, as it enables organizations to learn from the experiences of their counterparts in other industries and to identify commonalities and differences in compliance challenges. By sharing insights, lessons learned, and best practices, organizations can develop a more comprehensive understanding of the AI compliance landscape, allowing them to anticipate potential risks and adapt their strategies accordingly.

Additionally, organizations should collaborate with AI technology vendors, researchers, and developers to ensure that their AI systems are designed and implemented with compliance in mind. This may involve working closely with these stakeholders to incorporate transparency, accountability, and explainability features into AI models, or to develop advanced auditing and validation tools that can help organizations meet their compliance requirements.

A proactive and collaborative approach to AI compliance is essential for organizations to stay ahead of the curve in the rapidly evolving AI landscape. By fostering a proactive mindset and engaging in effective collaborations with industry peers, regulatory bodies, and other stakeholders, organizations can better anticipate and address emerging compliance challenges, ultimately driving AI compliance excellence and ensuring the responsible and ethical adoption of AI technologies across the industry.

About Jamie Culican
Author, Marketer, Publisher, Teacher

Jamie is a USA Today bestselling author with a passion for helping other authors succeed. She is the owner of Dragon Realm Press, a publishing house that specializes in working with indie authors. With over a decade of experience in the publishing industry, Jamie has become an expert in book marketing, book design, and book editing. Her approach is centered on creating a personalized and collaborative experience for her clients that results in high-quality, marketable books.

Her extensive marketing background allows her to guide authors through the complex world of book promotion, providing them with strategies that work. Jamie believes that every author has a unique voice, and she is committed to helping them share their stories with the world.

With a focus on innovation, Jamie has been at the forefront of integrating AI into the publishing industry. She believes that AI is a powerful tool that can help authors streamline their processes and reach new audiences. Jamie is passionate about helping authors navigate the ever-changing landscape of publishing and achieve their goals.

About Melle Melkumian

Author, Technologist, Marketer, Publisher

Melle has spent her career translating complex technology for the lay person, working with prestigious organizations such as NASA, Northrop Grumman, and Hewlett Packard. As the Marketing Director for an AI-enabled app company, Melle continues to leverage technology to drive meaningful change. She believes we are at a pivotal moment in history, where the incredible potential of AI is set to revolutionize the way we work and live. Melle is passionate about helping people navigate this shift and harness the power of AI to achieve their goals. Her expertise and unique perspective make her an invaluable resource for anyone looking to tap into the full potential of AI in their personal or professional life.

Outside of her professional career, Melle is a USA Today bestselling author, having published multiple books with rave reviews through a fresh approach to fantasy storytelling. Through her work as an author, Melle has gained a deep understanding of the writing and publishing process, and how emerging technologies like AI can support and enhance the creative process. She is excited to share her expertise and insights with fellow authors in the AI for Authors community.

About AI4CES

Empowering Professionals, Transforming Industries

AI4CES, the AI-focused educational platform designed to empower individuals across a wide range of vertical markets, including publishing, proposal and grant writing, and education. With our mission to make AI accessible to everyone, we provide comprehensive, tailored learning experiences through online classes, webinars, and more. Our expertly crafted courses break down complex AI concepts into digestible, easy-to-understand lessons, enabling you to harness the power of AI and revolutionize the way you work in your industry.

Don't miss the opportunity to stay ahead in today's competitive landscape by mastering AI with AI4CES. Our adaptive, engaging, and interactive learning modules ensure that you receive personalized, cutting-edge education in a format that suits your needs and preferences. Join the AI revolution with AI4CES and transform the way you approach challenges in your profession, from publishing to grant writing and beyond.

www.ai4cces.com

www.ingramcontent.com/pod-product-compliance
Lightning Source LLC
Chambersburg PA
CBHW060843220526
45466CB00003B/1225